SUE RYDER

SUE RYDER

A life lived for others

JOANNA BOGLE

GRACEWING

First published in England in 2022
by
Gracewing
2 Southern Avenue
Leominster
Herefordshire HR6 0QF
United Kingdom
www.gracewing.co.uk

ISBN 9780852449721

Typeset by Graceping

Cover design by Bernardita Peña Hurtado

Printed in the UK by Page Bros (Norwich) Ltd

CONTENTS

ACKNOWLEDGEMENTS

M Y WARMEST THANKS go to the Lady Ryder of Warsaw Memorial Trust for initiating this project, and to the individual members of the Trust who contributed their memories. Their support and encouragement throughout has been magnificent. In particular, I thank Dr Elizabeth Cheshire for her thoughtful and helpful checking of the whole text, and for her Foreword.

I am grateful to Cardinal Oswald Gracias, Archbishop of Bombay, for his help in obtaining information about the wedding of Sue Ryder and Leonard Cheshire, celebrated by his predecessor Cardinal Valerian Gracias. Thanks, too, to Alenka Lawrence for her recollections of staying with the Cheshires in the 1990s.

I would like to acknowledge everybody who kindly granted us permission to reproduce images, figures, and quotations throughout this text. Every effort was made to trace copyright holders, but we would be pleased to make suitable arrangements to clear permission for material reproduced in this book with any copyright holders whom it has not been possible to contact.

Finally, I thank Ann Welsh, my penfriend from Girl Guide days, who painstakingly went through the first draft of this book and made many useful notes and corrections: this book is affectionately dedicated to her with gratitude for our long friendship.

All photographs in this publication remain the property of the Lady Ryder of Warsaw Memorial Trust or Sue Ryder's family.

FOREWORD

WHEN THE TRUSTEES invited me to write a foreword for this biography of my mother Sue Ryder I was thrilled to have an opportunity to bring the story of her remarkable life to a new generation. Joanna Bogle has written a fast paced, factual and concise biography which brings my mother to life in the modern world and shows how relevant her ethos and everything that continues to be done in her name remain.

My mother spent her formative years in Yorkshire and Suffolk, the youngest of ten children. In her determination to join the war effort she added a year to her age (and never returned to her real age even decades after the war ended!), joining the First Aid Nursing Yeomanry (FANY) aged just fifteen and later the highly secret Special Operations Executive (SOE) formed by Winston Churchill. This took her to Italy and other occupied countries where she met and formed deep friendships with SOE agents, many of whom lost their young lives behind enemy lines.

Assigned to the Polish section of SOE, she formed a strong and lifelong bond with Poland.

These experiences and the horrors my mother witnessed visiting Nazi Concentration Camps shortly after their liberation had a profound effect on her and she dedicated the rest of her life to establishing a Living Memorial to relieve suffering worldwide. In the years after the ending of hostilities she worked tirelessly, often alone and at considerable personal risk in a war-ravaged Europe, establishing refuges for vulnerable displaced people across Europe and brought others back to live in her mother's home in Suffolk. Her drive and determination to build a better peace and everything she achieved are all the more extraordinary considering she was still only in her early twenties.

Her mother's house in Suffolk, originally a Tudor farmhouse, was extended and converted over subsequent years to meet the needs of the growing community, often with volunteers and donated materials, eventually becoming home to thirty or so residents (affectionately known as Bods), and many more secretarial staff, volunteers and carers. It became the Headquarters of the Forgotten Allies Trust and later the Sue Ryder Foundation.

In this, the Sue Ryder Home in Cavendish, my brother Jeromy and I were born in the early 1960s. It was an unconventional upbringing but very happy one and an immense privilege growing up with survivors of concentration camps, refugees from post war Europe and those who came to care for them.

Our family lived in two small rooms upstairs eating our meals on a folding table on the landing, and spent many happy summer evenings playing cricket in the garden with Bods and volunteers or fishing for carp and (in my brother's case) frog spawn in the pond. The pond was a central part of our childhood—my brother narrowly escaped a severe telling off after pushing the old wooden rowing boat away from the jetty when a nanny looking after us while our parents were abroad had one foot in the boat and one on the jetty, resulting in a cold and unexpected dip, by offering to put the kettle on. Our parents were away for many months of every year visiting homes and projects worldwide and we grew used to their absences and the joy of their homecoming.

My mother had great compassion for a number of young men who had been imprisoned in post-war Europe, many of whom had witnessed atrocities and sought revenge against Nazi perpetrators who subsequently escaped justice and were themselves sentenced to life and some to death. She visited them every year and petitioned for their release and rehabilitation. These visits usually took place in mid-December and she would drive all night across Europe to be home in time to celebrate a traditional Polish Christmas with the Bods. One of these men came to live with us at Cavendish following his release.

Our mother's absences, all that was done by her or in her name and the diverse community we lived in seemed quite normal to us as children.

Reading the second section of this book and in later life I have realised the full extent of her work and how extraordinary it was. My parents had an unshakable belief that if everyone cooperated in a common aim—as people had done during the war—great things could be achieved for the common good and this, together with their strong Christian faith, guided their lives and all they did.

The countries my mother worked in and the homes and projects she founded are vast in number. A great many of them continue to this day, almost a century after her birth, and I must thank the trustees of LRWMT, her legacy, for putting this index together. It is impossible to estimate how many have been helped or have volunteered in some way.

The photos are from her archive or personal to the family, many released for the first time for publication in this biography.

My mother never sought publicity or wanted to talk about what she did and was often secretive even with family, possibly a lasting effect of her SOE training combined with her unassuming nature, and was famously annoyed when she unexpectedly found herself the subject of "This is Your Life" on national television, but I feel certain she would have been immensely proud of all those who have taken up her calling and continued the work started in her name.

I really hope you enjoy this book as much as I did and that together we can mark my mother's centenary by continuing to act and think as she did throughout her life—helping the person next to us.

With best wishes

Elizabeth Cheshire

TIMELINE

1924	Sue Ryder is born on the 3rd July in Leeds, Yorkshire.
1930s	The Ryder family move permanently to their home in Thurlow, Suffolk. Sue attends Benenden School, Kent.
1939/1940	Sue joins the First Aid Nursing Yeomanry (FANY) and is seconded to the Special Operations Executive (SOE).
1945-1951	Relief work with the Anglo-French European Units, the Red Cross and the Guide International Service, while at the same time, working alone visiting prisons and hospitals.
1951 onwards	Continues the Prison visiting and social work alone, after the relief organisations have withdrawn.
1952	Sue launches the Holiday Scheme, initially in Denmark and then the UK.
1953	Sue registers the Living Memorial with the Charity Commission in the UK, initially as The Forgotten Allies Friendship Trust, which later becomes the Sue Ryder Foundation, and is now simply Sue Ryder.

1953	She buys her mother's house in the village of Cavendish in Suffolk and this becomes the first Sue Ryder Home in the UK and the Headquarters.
1956	Sue appears on 'This is your Life' on BBC Television.
1957	St Christopher's, a Home near Hanover in Germany, is established.
1957	The first Sue Ryder Home in Poland is established at Konstancin.
1957	Sue is awarded the Order of the British Empire (OBE).
1958	Together with Leonard Cheshire, Sue establishes the Ryder-Cheshire Mission for the relief of suffering.
1959	Sue marries Leonard Cheshire.
1959	Together they found the Ryder-Cheshire Centre at Dehra Dun, called 'Raphael' and then visit Australia and New Zealand to encourage fundraising for 'Raphael'.
1960	The second Home in the UK is started at Hickleton Hall, Yorkshire.
1969	The third Home in the UK is started at Stagenhoe, near Hitchin in Hertfordshire.
1960s-1970s	Many Homes are established in Poland and Yugoslavia.

1970s	Half-way houses start in Belgium
1976	Sue is appointed a Companion of the Order of St Michael and St George (CMG).
1978	Sue Ryder is created a Life Peer, as Baroness Ryder of Warsaw and Cavendish.
1970s–1990s	Many Sue Ryder Homes are started in the UK.
1980s	2-year project in Belize.
1982	Establishment of the Sue Ryder Foundation in Ireland.
1984	Founding of the Sue Ryder Prayer Fellowship.
1985	Sue works in Ethiopia.
1990	Establishment of the Sue Ryder Foundation in Malawi.
1994	Registration of the Sue Ryder Foundation in Prague, Czech Republic. Although the work could not be registered until this year, Sue had been working in what had been Czechoslovakia since the 1950s.
1997	Establishment of the Fondazione Sue Ryder in Italy.
1998	St Katharine's Parmoor is handed over to the Sue Ryder Prayer Fellowship.

2000	Bouverie Foundation, now the Lady Ryder of Warsaw Memorial Trust, is established.
2000	Start of the Ryder-Cheshire Foundation's work in Timor-Leste.
2000	Sue Ryder dies on 2nd November.
2009	Opening of the Lady Ryder of Warsaw rooms at the Polish Catholic Mission House at 'Bellevue', Lourdes.
2024	Centenary of Sue Ryder's birth.

Part One
The Biography

1 A LOVING HOME

THE BRITAIN INTO which Margaret Susan Ryder was born on July 3rd 1924[1] was one that was deeply marked by the Great War (1914–18) that had concluded a few years earlier, but was, in many ways unchanged from the era of Queen Victoria who had died some twenty years before.

It was a Britain with a strong sense of history, sombre cities, strong industries and busy sea-ports, growing suburbs, and acres of countryside dotted with farms and small villages. Family structures were strong and divorce rare. Christianity was widely practised and Sunday church attendance regarded as the norm.

Britain ruled a vast overseas empire, which included all of what is today India, Pakistan, Myanmar and Bangladesh, along with most of Africa south of the Sahara, and all of Singapore and Malaya. The great dominions of Australia, Canada and New Zealand were also part of this empire, and British people felt proud of all of this and confident in the Empire's stability.

The official school-leaving age had recently been raised to 14. Many people earned their living "in service" as cooks, maids or gardeners in others' households. Electricity was a new arrival for lighting or powering equipment, and most homes were still lit by gas or lamplight, and heated by open fires.

---

[1] When she applied to join the First Aid Nursing Yeomanry, Sue Ryder gave her birth date as 1923 in order to claim to be over 16 as the regulations required, and this date was frequently quoted in later material written about her, and in her own autobiography *Child of My Love* published in 1997. 1924 is the correct date.

This was a Britain without motorways, television, computers or mobile phones, where pizzas and "fast food" were unknown. Air travel had just begun, but for most people was something utterly remote. In the countryside much farm work was still done with horses. A network of railways connected towns, cities and villages: few people owned cars.

The Ryder family had two manor houses, at Scarcroft near Leeds and at Great Thurlow in Suffolk, and divided their time between the two. Susan was the youngest of ten children. Her father, Charles Foster Ryder, was a man of the Victorian age, born in 1856. He owned and farmed two large estates, and was a director of Tetleys, a major brewing firm. By his first wife Anna he had five children,[2] and in 1911, widowed, he married Mabel Simms, the daughter of an Anglican clergyman, and Sue was their youngest child. By the time of Sue's birth, he was an established figure as local landowner and squire at Scarcroft where the family accepted the status and responsibilities of their position as a matter of course.

Sue—which is how she was always known and will be named in this book—would recall a formal, structured household, with the children having a separate life in the nursery under an "extremely strict nanny", but allowed downstairs for Sunday lunch and "a cold supper to which we helped ourselves as the staff had the evening off".[3] From the age of eight, they joined their parents for other meals too. Her father, already middle-aged when she was born, began every day with a cold bath, invariably wore a high

---

[2]   These were Sue Ryder's half-brothers and sisters: Charles, Daniel, Rosamund, Agnes and William. She had three full brothers, John, Michael and Stephen and a sister, Mary.

[3]   S. Ryder, *Child of My Love* (London: Collins Harvill, 1986, 1997), p. 8. As this book will be quoted frequently, future references will be to the initials CML in brackets in the text.

stiff collar and was "quiet and reserved, spending more time in working on the family farms and in reading and writing, than in talking" (CML, 7). But he was a figure of affection and the family was a united one. Sue, as the youngest, had perhaps the easiest and most relaxed relationship with him. She recalled riding with her father to visit the various farms on the estate and talking about books and history and world events.

Although the family owned large amounts of land, they were not well-off, as farming was not highly profitable in these difficult years of the 1920s and 30s, and much of their time was spent in attempting to relieve poverty among their tenants, and among the back streets and tenements of Leeds.

Sue grew up knowing about the tragedy of war: her half-brother, William, had been killed in 1917 at just twenty years old, while serving with the Royal Flying Corps. A memorial to him had been placed at St Peter's church near the family's Suffolk home at Great Thurlow, and Charles Ryder wore a black tie in mourning for him for the rest of his life. The idea of service and sacrifice was part of the whole atmosphere of the Ryder family homes, along with that of care for the poor and responsibility for the community.

Religion was central to life: Mabel Ryder went to Holy Communion daily and the Church's seasons were observed with sweets renounced during Lent and Sundays celebrated as specifically different from any other day in the week. As members of the Church of England, the Ryders worshipped in ancient churches with Saxon and Norman roots, with history, traditions and faith bound together. At their home at Scarcroft, any wandering homeless people were invited in for baths and meals and given clothing and other help.

Sue Ryder's mother, Mabel Ryder

Throughout her life, the Christian faith would be central to Sue Ryder: from earliest childhood she was taught to begin and end each day with prayer, and to seek God's help and guidance for decisions. She was familiar with the Scriptures, read aloud to her at home and in church, and understood that God was the author of life, and had come to live among men in the person of Jesus Christ, dying on the Cross and rising again for man's redemption. For her, this was not just a belief that had shaped Britain's culture and laws, but a living reality, giving meaning and purpose to life's journey, and answering the deepest questions about humanity's existence. The habits of prayer taught at home remained with her, and over the years she would pray and take part in Sunday worship in unfamiliar places and situations, but always with deep commitment.

The Ryder family life was a rural one: Sue learned how to make butter in the dairy and earned pocket-money caring for hens and selling the eggs (she spent the money on a crucifix). Everyone helped with harvesting and long years later Sue would recall the "shocking" of sheaves of corn, working "from daybreak until the light faded". It was hard work but in a countryside where chemical sprays and mechanised farming were unknown, there was also great beauty: "the smell of the corn under the blue August sky and the sight of the clover, poppies and cornflowers, the hedges with hips and haws ... blackberries ripening and the smell of the horses with their jingling harness" (CML 12).

Sue as a dairymaid at the family's home in Suffolk

Every year the family moved from their Yorkshire home to their Suffolk one, reserving a railway carriage to transport themselves, their staff, and large amounts of luggage. The staff had their own hierarchy and structured life, each day beginning with prayers, meals eaten formally, (the elevated status of the housekeeper meant that she had her meal in her own room), and uniforms worn by the maids as they went about their tasks to a strict timetable beginning with early morning tea served to guests. The maids' uniforms were pink cotton with mob caps in the morning, and black with frilly aprons in the afternoon (CML 18).

The financial hardships of the 1930s with many out of work and unable to pay rents, eventually brought about a major change for the Ryder family. Charles Ryder had been helping as many tenants and local people as possible but eventually it became clear that he could not maintain two estates. Yorkshire had to be given up, the family moving permanently to Thurlow in Suffolk.

Throughout her childhood, Sue was close to her brothers and sister and enjoyed their company, with farm work, games, and treats such as camping out overnight in the grounds of their home. But the overriding influence on her was her mother. Mabel Ryder not only taught her daughter at home rather than sending her to school for the first years of education, but also took her regularly on visits to the impoverished families she was helping in Leeds and in the Suffolk countryside. Seeing the efforts of people to keep clean in dirty overcrowded tenements or to cope courageously with permanent disability while marooned in an upstairs room in a country village, made deep and unforgettable impressions on the young Sue. Working to alleviate poverty and suffering was central to the weekly routines of her childhood, along with acquiring the required skills in cooking and cleaning: scrubbing floors remained a passion throughout her long life. This was an era when social distinctions were still very much observed—she recalled an elderly village woman "bobbing" a curtsey to the Ryder family car before accepting an offered lift—but the Ryder family style was very much one of genuine efforts to serve the community and offer practical help whenever possible.

With such close family bonds, it was unsurprising that when sent as a weekly boarder to school, the young Sue was desperately homesick. She would later recall that she wept every night and found it difficult to explain to anyone why she was so unhappy. She found solace in music and in dancing, but the experience remained with her as a miserable one.

Things changed when she was old enough to attend a school that would mark her for the rest of her life—Benenden. This had been recently established and was regarded as forward-looking and progressive as its founders assumed that the girls would go on to have careers and to be active in public and community life. Women had been given the vote in 1918 and many had perforce to work as family breadwinners following the deaths of menfolk in the war.

At Benenden there was an emphasis on training in public speaking and on taking up hobbies and acquiring useful skills. The tone seems to have been hearty and patriotic, with a strong message of service to others. Years later Sue would say the school "had a marvellous spirit about it"[4] and loved to quote the school prayer which asked that "there may go forth from this place a great company who strengthened by Thy grace and inspired by Thy spirit shall serve thee faithfully, for the welfare of their fellow-men and for the honour of Thy great name ..."

---

[4]   Interview with Sue Ryder, Imperial War Museum sound archives.

Sue Ryder as a young girl at about the time she started at Benenden school

It was an uncomplicated and practical message. When war broke out in 1939, the 15-year-old Sue, at church that Sunday morning of September 3rd with her family in Great Thurlow, assumed that the call to "serve Thee faithfully" had arrived and lost little time in getting involved. She would later say that she and her friends were "infuriated" that Britain seemed so weak and unarmed and had "betrayed" the men who had died in the First World War: she believed that successive governments had "failed to expose what the Nazis were doing ... for us it seemed that the war was inevitable."[5]

---

[5]   Interview with Sue Ryder, Imperial War Museum sound archives.

2 WAR

ONE OF THE first things that brought home to many people in Britain the reality of war was the evacuation of children from the major cities to the safer countryside. This was done in expectation of immediate massive air raids from Germany's Luftwaffe. In fact, the air raids did not start immediately—but the impact of evacuation was considerable.

Many of the children who were brought out to the countryside—gathered together at railway stations, each child wearing a label—were from extremely poor backgrounds and were dirty, under-nourished and carrying fleas. Some had never slept in a bed and flatly refused to do so, believing that beds were only for dead people. Some had only ever slept three to a bed, and had never seen sheets.

Often the host families, comfortably-off in rural areas, were appalled and shocked. Not so Sue Ryder and her mother, who were already familiar with the conditions of the urban slums of Leeds.

Sue left school in the summer of 1939 and seems to have been absolutely in her element as she immediately went to train as a nurse. She would later recall:

> Evacuees from London were given rooms in our home, and for a few months I worked in a local hospital where the simple training and subsequent examinations proved extremely useful in the wards and even more so in later life. Quite a number of evacuees from the East End [of London] were admitted, many of them children who were frightened they might never see their homes or parents again. The majority had never had the opportunity

> of seeing the country before. They came from slum
> areas and were used to sharing a bed. Some we had
> to persuade to change their clothes and many were
> infected so that on admission their heads were
> tooth-combed with carbolic ... (CML 52).

Nursing in that era was strictly regimented, with rules about the length of the uniform skirt (mid-calf) the colour of stockings (black) and etiquette at a formal meeting with Matron (sleeves rolled down to wrist, cotton cuffs removed and replaced with starched linen ones). There were communal meals with Grace said beforehand, and structured regulations about the cleaning of patients' lockers and aligning of beds.[1]

Sue seems to have relished this environment, with a daily start before 6am, three minutes allowed for making each patient's bed, and much scrubbing of mackintosh mattress-covers and sterilising of medical equipment.

But she wanted to be more active. A National Service Act had now been passed which established the calling-up of all men and women from the age of 18 for some form of war work, and girls were joining the armed forces. Sue would later recall that she was "horrified" by the idea of being called up; she wanted to volunteer.[2]

For a girl from her background, the First Aid Nursing Yeomanry (FANY) was an obvious choice. The FANY had been established during the Boer War[3] as a private initiative: young women who joined bought their own uniforms and volunteered for what was initially a mounted unit aimed at bringing wounded men more quickly from the battlefield. In the summer of 1914 it was revived by a group

---

[1]   A flavour of this can be gained from M. Dickens, *One Pair of Feet* (London: Penguin, 1976).

[2]   Interview with Sue Ryder, Imperial War Museum sound archives.

[3]   The Second Boer War, 1899–1902

of women who, without apparently seeking official permission, crossed the Channel from Folkestone to offer nursing help in Belgium and became attached to the Belgian Army.

By the 1930s stories of the FANY's work in the First World War had earned them honours, and a tradition had been established. But it was not an ordinary unit: in its first years FANYs paid a donation to join and it was assumed that they knew how to ride and came from families who owned land and horses. By 1939 it was part of the British Army. There was no formal class barrier, but it carried a style and atmosphere of its own that was generally recognised.

It was natural that Sue Ryder of the manor house, Great Thurlow, would gravitate towards the FANYs. But she was only able to do so by misrepresenting her age, telling them that she was 16 when in fact she was a year younger. Long into her old age, when it was no longer remotely necessary, she would maintain the fiction that she was born in 1923 when in fact it was 1924.

From the summer of 1940, when she first put on the FANY's uniform—khaki skirt and jacket, and cap with its circled Maltese Cross badge— Sue would be proud of having served with the First Aid Nursing Yeomanry, and with good reason, as it provided some of the bravest women in active service. Through the FANY, Sue would work with men and women who were sent into occupied Europe to work with resistance groups against the Nazis.

The initial three weeks were spent learning drill at Ketteringham in Norfolk. The young women were expected to march correctly, under the direction of a sergeant from the Devonshire Regiment whose commands Sue would later recall as being difficult to understand due to his strong accent. They were inspected daily by their Commanding Officer, Ethel Boileau, who in civilian life had been a well-known author. She was the owner of the manor house where they were based. Standards were high, although the girls slept in tents and there were no luxuries. Shoes had to be gleaming with polish, as did the Sam Browne belt[4]. Hair had to be up well above the shirt collar.

Sue Ryder in lorry cab in FANY uniform

---

[4]   The Sam Browne belt is the standard leather belt and strap worn by officers in the British Army.

There was a strong *esprit de corps*, and the girls were conscious of belonging to something special. In many cases their families also knew each other, and there were bonds of social connections and a shared sense of wanting to uphold the honour and tradition of the FANY.

It was very much an Army unit. Addressed by their surnames only, the girls worked hard, learning first aid and stretcher skills, map reading, night driving, and mechanics. Every FANY was expected to know how to maintain and clean the vehicles she was learning to drive, from a car to a seven-ton lorry.

Sue was now earning eleven shillings and twopence a week—about 56p in today's money—which at that time would pay for snacks, bus fares, and personal necessities[5]. On this pay, and as a teenager who had been a schoolgirl only a few months before, she was ordered to report to the headquarters of the Special Operations Executive (SOE) in London's Baker Street. She arrived in "some trepidation"[6] as a friend had said that this—known to the FANY as "Bingham's Unit"—was involved in secret work[7]. SOE was formed in July 1940[8], after the British Army's rescue from Dunkirk, when Britain stood alone facing occupied Europe.

---

[5]   In 1940 a bottle of shampoo cost sixpence (approx. 3p) and a packet of Maltesers twopence (approx. 1p).

[6]   Interview with Sue Ryder, Imperial War Museum sound archives.

[7]   Mrs Bingham , married to the son of a former American ambassador to Britain, carried out the initial recruitment interviews before the war in the vicarage of St Paul's church, Wilton Place London SW1.

[8]   SOE was run by an Operation Chief, always known as "CD". At the time Sue Ryder began work for the organisation the Chief was Air Commodore Frank Nelson. He was succeeded by Sir Charles Hambro, who in 1942 was succeeded by Major General Colin McVean Gubbins. His deputy was Lt General Harry Sporborg, who in later years would work closely with Sue Ryder as the Chairman of her Foundation.

Its effective founder was Dr Hugh Dalton, the Minister of Economic Warfare, who suggested "a new organisation to co-ordinate, inspire, control and assist the nationals of the oppressed countries who must themselves be the direct participants. We need absolute secrecy, a certain fanatical enthusiasm, willingness to work with the different nationalities, complete political reliability."[9] The aim was

> to encourage and enable the peoples of the occupied countries to harass the German war effort at every possible point by sabotage, subversion, go-slow practices etc, and at the same time to build up secret forces therein, organised, armed and trained to take their part only when the final assault began…in its simplest terms, this involved the ultimate delivery to occupied territory of large numbers of personnel and quantities of arms and explosives.[10]

There were separate sections dealing with the different occupied countries and secrecy was such that none knew about any of the others.

Sue was sent initially to the Czech section, Station 17, based at Brickendonbury, near Hertford, a house formerly owned by Lord Curzon which had become a preparatory school before being taken over for use by SOE. Here the work was mostly driving, ferrying the agents—nicknamed "Bods"—to the stations for what might be a secret mission. Information was never swapped nor were destinations discussed. She recalled the Colonel in charge at Brickendonbury as being extremely strict, and there was a constant emphasis on secrecy. The young women working

---

[9]   Hugh Dalton, *The Fateful Years*, quoted in John Grehan and Martin Mace, *Unearthing Churchill's Secret Army* (Barnsley: Pen and Sword, 2012).

[10] Major Gen Colin McVean Gubbins, writing in 1943, quoted in Grehan and Mace, *Unearthing Churchill's Secret Army*.

there were not allowed out, and things often felt claustro-
phobic: they occasionally sneaked out for cycle rides, using
folding bicycles designed to be packed and dropped by
parachute to agents in occupied countries. The Czech
section had been involved in the assassination of leading
Nazi Reinhard Heydrich, one of the architects of the
slaughter of millions of Jewish people.[11]

In later life Sue maintained the rules of secrecy with
regard to her work for SOE and while deeply and permanently marked by her involvement—and dedicating her
life to honouring the memory of those who had made
sacrifices—she never revealed anything about the operations or the people she trained. Among those now known
to have trained at Brickendonbury were Odette Sansom—
whose story later became a successful film—and French
agent Jack Danby.

After a few weeks with the Czechs, Sue was sent on a
training course for coding and shooting where she met
Bods from various sections including French Canadians
working for the French section, who had been involved in
the Dieppe raid, and Norwegians involved in the raids
against the "heavy water" weaponry.

She was then posted to the Polish section, at Audley
End House, a Jacobean mansion near Saffron Walden in
Essex, listed by SOE as STS 43. Thus was to begin a deep
involvement with Poland, and a love for Polish people that
would last for decades and result in her, in later life, taking
the name of Poland's capital city to be part of her own.

Today Audley End House is in the care of English
Heritage, and visitors flock to see the stately rooms and

---

[11]   Training films for SOE were later made at Brickendonbury and
are now at the Imperial War Museum. It also featured in an
official film *Now it can be Told* shown at the end of the war, and
in a TV programme *The Secret War* in the 1970s. A commemo-
rative plaque was placed at the house in 2010.

Victorian children's nursery. But its wartime history is also noted. The house was requisitioned for military purposes in March 1941 following the death of its last owner, Lord Braybrook, and was initially used by the Army. In October of that year it was handed over to SOE for the training of Polish parachutists, jointly commanded by a British and a Polish officer.

Here the Poles were trained in sabotage techniques and weaponry, and were equipped with everything they would need for their secret missions. One room was set aside for making authentic Polish clothing, another for producing the necessary documents. Guns and munitions were stored in the basement. The great hall was used for lectures and there was also a billiards room and mess rooms for eating and relaxing. There was an assault course in the grounds and the men practised hazardous river crossings on the river Cam. Everything was kept secret: if local people were baffled by the occasional sounds of explosives or gunfire they tended not to speak about it.[12] The Polish officers who trained at Audley End would later be known as the "Silent Unseen".

Today a memorial in the grounds of Audley End House commemorates the men who trained there and gave their lives. Staff gather at the memorial annually on November 11th.

Poland presented in one sense an uncomplicated picture for Britain. Unlike France, where the Vichy regime had co-operated with the Nazis, Poland was united in opposition. The country's very existence had been formally destroyed, with part absorbed into the German Reich, a central area known as the General Government, and the Eastern parts taken by the Soviet Union which had invaded on September 17th 1939 while the country's army was fighting the Germans.

---

[12]   Information from English Heritage, 2021

But in another sense the relationship with Britain was complicated. The Poles had had to fight the Red Army just twenty years earlier on the outskirts of Warsaw to defend their country's independence.[13] They distrusted the USSR and were wary of Britain's willingness to co-operate with the Soviets. Polish agents used prudence in sharing information and codes with the British authorities and kept a measured distance. They insisted on having their own independent radio transmitters and codes. Future events would prove their wariness well-founded. As one commentator has noted:

> British voices declared their determination to see, one day, a strong and independent Poland, but this took no account of the predator on her eastern border. The Soviet Union had, after all, effectively been an ally of Germany for nearly two years, before she was invaded in June 1941 and only then embarked on her huge sacrifices in the 'Great Patriotic War'. It was left to Poland's underground press, rather than Britain's largely pro-Soviet newspapers, to declare the true nature of Stalin's rule.[14]

Every one of the Polish agents had an extraordinary story of survival and escape. Sue would long remember "Zub", who had fought in the September campaign against the invading German forces, escaped from subsequent German captivity and joined a Resistance group which worked to rescue Jews in the Cracow area. A fellow member of his group was a young worker in a stone quarry, who was training secretly to become a priest—his name was Karol Wojtyla and he would later become Pope—now

---

[13]   The army of the fledgling Polish republic defeated the Red Army in 1920 in what Poles today still describe as the "miracle on the Vistula".

[14]   Jonathan Walker, *Poland Alone: Britain SOE and the collapse of Polish Resistance, 1944* (Stroud: The History Press, 2008), p. 22.

Saint—John Paul II. Zub later undertook a mission with the Resistance to Budapest and from there was helped to escape to Britain via Yugoslavia, Italy and France.

In Britain, Zub worked with another officer "Kitwicz" arranging flights to occupied Poland dropping agents and supplies to Resistance groups. It was the job of Sue and her colleagues in the FANY working with SOE to prepare agents for departure on these flights: they went through every item of clothing and all personal toilet articles to ensure there were no British labels, and checked that all the equipment, (including forged papers, a revolver, and money), were in order. All agents were also given a poison tablet to take if, when captured, they felt they were in danger of giving away information under torture. This tablet was usually sewn into the shirt collar.

"Though the pre-mission hours were naturally very tense, there was also a wonderful sense of humour and cheerfulness amongst the Bods" Sue would later write (CML 76) recalling how the Poles would crack jokes and rally one another—and how they were also very devout. Before a mission, a priest would be asked to come to the station so that each man could go to confession.

Sue and her colleagues prepared food for the Bods to eat on the long flight, with flasks of coffee—this would be the last meal they would enjoy before being dropped into occupied territory and a dangerous uncertain future.

Some of the Bods had come from concentration camps in Siberia, to which they had been deported by the Soviet invaders of Poland in September 1939 and from where they had finally been released following the Sikorski-Stalin pact of July 1941. This pact, which followed the German invasion of the USSR, enabled them to join an army under General Anders to fight the Nazis. They had left behind many other Poles who had been unable to reach the various gathering centres. Some were later formed into a Soviet-led unit, others perished in the network of gulag camps. The stories the Bods told of the Siberian camps were horrific: families were split up and children became lost, thousands of people had died, and some had resorted to cannibalism through hunger.

The Poles living and working together in SOE forged a strong community: they were young and far from their own homes and mostly had no knowledge of what had happened to their families. They were well aware that the future of their country was very uncertain: the Soviets were imposing a rule that was just as terrifying as that of the Nazis. Sue never forgot a wartime Christmas with these men: they enthusiastically took over the kitchen and using their British rations produced a traditional Polish "Wigilia" meal, with beetroot soup and a variety of fish dishes. Hay was placed on the table to recall Christ's birth in a stable, and the traditional *oplatek* wafer was broken and distributed.[15] Polish and English carols were sung, and at midnight a priest arrived to celebrate Mass. One of the Poles gave Sue his parachute badge, with a written note "Until we meet at the Central Station in Warsaw" (CML 77).

Sue was still in her teens. She was working with men who knew they faced grave danger and possibly death. Her contacts with her own family were by letter. The only

---

[15] The Christmas wafer (Polish: opłatek,) is a Catholic Christmas tradition celebrated in Poland, Lithuania, and Slovakia. Before partaking of the Christmas Eve meal, the family gathers around the table. The eldest member holds a large wafer and breaks off a piece to begin the ritual. The remaining wafer is passed on to another member while a prayer for loved ones is said. This continues until everyone at the table has a piece of the wafer. Finally, each family member gives wishes to every other family member, consuming a piece of wafer broken off from the wafer piece of the person to whom they were giving their wishes.

address they could use was "Room 98, Horseguards, London SW1" and mail from there was collected regularly by courier and distributed to the various SOE stations. Sue's father died in 1942 and the family home at Thurlow was sold; her mother moved to another house nearby. The years of manor house life with uniformed maids and the routine of the countryside seasons were slipping away.

Sue spent some time at Pollards Park House, near Chalfont St Giles in Buckinghamshire, STS 20A. From here, as at Audley End, agents were sent to Poland and messages received. Courageous Poles succeeded in sending to Britain information about what was happening in Auschwitz, and the planned extermination of millions of Jewish people, and also information about the V2 weapons Germany was building.

At Chalfont St Giles, Sue shared a room for some days with a Polish courier Elzbieta Zawacka, whose English name, adopted to cover her identity, was Elizabeth Watson. She had already taken part in several dangerous assignments and found her way to Britain from Poland via Spain bringing documents for the Polish government in exile. She was waiting to be flown back to Poland and in due course would go on to take part in the 1944 Warsaw Uprising. Already she knew that one of her brothers, Egon, had died in a concentration camp and that her sister Kiara was imprisoned. Later she would learn that her brother-in-law was among the Polish officers murdered by the Soviets at Katyn.[16] It was the courage of people like this who would

---

[16]   See Bernard O'Connor, *Elzbieta Zawacka: Polish soldier, courier and secret agent*, paper at St Mary's University, Twickenham, London. The Katyn massacre was a mass murder of nearly 22,000 Polish military officers and intelligentsia prisoners of war carried out by the Soviet Union, specifically the NKVD ("People's Commissariat for Internal Affairs", the Soviet secret police) in April and May 1940.

inspire Sue not only during the war years but afterwards, as she sought to perpetuate their memory and honour their sacrifices. Working with the Bods shaped Sue Ryder's life, and she was inspired by their courage, humour, tolerance, faith and cheerfulness:

> Though books or films about SOE often catch the tension involved in the work, they rarely recapture the dreadful fear and anguish that most of the Bods, if not all, experienced. The romance which is invariably introduced into such works seems out of place. We had those platonic friendships which people say are impossible: they do not seem to realise what such friendships really mean, nor the necessity for them (CML 105).

When she looked back to the War, it was always the Bods that she remembered, and all of her post-war work was done to commemorate them, especially those who died unknown, or in some grim forgotten prison after torture. In their name, she created a "Living Memorial", trying to heal suffering and offer comfort and assistance to anyone in need.

> To live and share, however briefly, the lives of great, yet unknown people made a profound impression on me and I felt it was a privilege never to be forgotten (CML 78).

3 OVERSEAS

I N 1943, AT very short notice, Sue was told she was being posted overseas. She and her friend Diana, "Dipsy" Portman travelled to London together after they had been given some days leave to be with their families.

Sue spent her week's leave in Thurlow with her mother, who saw how exhausted she was and treated her to plenty of rest, with breakfast in bed in the mornings (CML 209). Then, with Dipsy and another girl, Pammy, she reported to London where they were given rooms in a bomb-damaged hotel near the FANY headquarters opposite St Paul's church in Wilton Place. Sue's mother then met her in London on the final day before departure overseas, and they prayed together in St Paul's church. They would not meet again until the war ended in 1945.

Sue and Dipsy both believed that they were heading for Eastern Europe, and excitedly checked over their uniforms, including their formal greatcoats—very smart with scarlet lining and deep cuffs—which they hoped to wear at the victory parade in Warsaw. There was a briefing about a possible plan for the Western allies to break through the Danube gap ahead of the Red Army, but this seemed unrealistic, as it was already clear that the Americans trusted the Soviets and would not do anything to impede their progress.

The two girls spent some time in Jermyn Street in the West End, using their last hours of free time to visit the luxury shops. With little money to spend, they tried out a free scent spray at a cosmetic counter, and listened at a record shop in Bond Street to Rachmaninov and Brahms.

They then reported as ordered to Addison Road station in Kensington.[1] Their destination—in a blacked-out train—was Liverpool where after a long slow journey they were kept waiting for some hours in a damp warehouse before being marched aboard a ship carrying their kitbags.

They soon realised that there was no question of their being part of a liberating force in Eastern Europe—their destination was North Africa. It was a long, hot journey and six women shared a small cabin originally designed for one, but felt themselves fortunate compared to the soldiers crowded below decks in even more cramped conditions.

The next stage of the war for Sue would be Tunis where she stayed for a short time of which she later had two main memories: one was the opportunity of having a bath, the water being brought by two German prisoners-of-war from the Afrika Corps who told her they were certain of their country's victory, and the other was being seriously unwell from infected mosquito bites. From Tunis she was flown with three other girls to Italy, where in primitive conditions—some orange boxes covered with a blanket to serve as a bed, some pieces of canvas to offer partial privacy for the hole they dug in the ground as a lavatory— they faced a freezing winter. Tents were blown down in ferocious winds, water in makeshift hot-water-bottles froze at night, and blinding blizzards made all travel difficult. The FANY's main job was driving, and maintaining their vehicles made for sleepless nights as the engines needed to be started up every twenty minutes to prevent the diesel from freezing.

Sue Ryder married during the war, but her husband was killed in action not long afterwards. Sue never spoke of

---

[1]   This station had been bombed in 1940 and was only used for troop movements and freight trains. It was rebuilt after the war and is now named Kensington Olympia.

this wartime marriage, perhaps because it was kept secret, FANY officers at that time being forbidden to marry without Army permission. She may also have felt that, along with many aspects of her wartime career, it was somehow under a general blanket of secrecy through the Official Secrets Act which she had signed on joining SOE. In addition, at that time it was illegal to marry under the age of 21 without parental permission,[2] which may have been impossible to obtain under wartime conditions. After the war Sue was registered as a widow and received a war widow's pension, and her marriage certificate, in 1959, lists her status as a widow. Even her future children never learned the identity of her first husband.

It is clear that this wartime loss added to her already strong conviction of the importance of commemorating those who had given their lives, with "remembrance" the theme of her future charity work, a symbol of rosemary is its symbol, and the idea of a "Living Memorial" as its inspiration.

All of 1944 was certainly a sad time. The Allies were fighting their way up through Italy, and Sue would later write bleakly of mistakes made through political decisions that cost lives at Monte Cassino and elsewhere. She was also introduced, in rural areas of Italy, to poverty and hardship beyond anything she had seen in Britain, with outbreaks of typhus and other diseases. Her driving took her past areas where battles had been fought, and unburied bodies lay blackening in the streets and were eaten by rats at night. The work involved treating men from the Italian anti-Mussolini partisans, who had been hiding in the forests and suffered from gangrenous wounds.

---

[2]   The legal age was changed to 18 with the Family Law Reform Act 1969.

By June 1944 she was in Rome with other jubilant Allied forces. Her memories of that time range from the "incredible sensation" of sleeping between proper sheets in a real bed, to an audience with Pope Pius XII and walks to explore churches and outlying villages in warm sunshine. She wrote to a friend about the extraordinary contrasts of ugliness and beauty, death and suffering, along with mountains in springtime, wild flowers, and music. "You or I may possibly still be here on earth when the present struggle finally ends and the next stage of our life, which will certainly include relief work, begins. Each of us has a time limit on earth and so it is up to us to make the most of our lives while we are here..." (CML 126)

Sue was now twenty years old. This period of her life was one that involved death and sorrow as constant companions. There was a particularly acute loss when newly-married Dipsy and her husband were killed near Florence. Sue found the loss hard to bear: "I kept thinking it must be someone else and that I could go and discuss it all with her still". (CML 129).

The war was still not over: in August 1944, crews of the Royal Air Force—including Polish pilots at Brindisi—were taking off to fly to Warsaw in attempts to give supplies to the Polish Home Army (*Armia Krajowa*). This was the famous Warsaw Uprising—now commemorated annually in the city with a solemn Two Minutes of Silence—in which the Home Army rose to hold the city as the Germans were preparing to retreat in the wake of defeats on the Eastern Front and the D-day landings in France. The Poles fought with courage—but the USSR, after issuing radio broadcasts encouraging the Rising, deliberately held its Red Army back on the eastern shores of the river Vistula, so that the Germans retained the city and over two months of fighting reduced it to ruins, leaving the Red Army to invade in due course.[3]

Many of the RAF flights failed to get through—the flight was long and much of it over enemy territory—and making an accurate drop over a city where the territory controlled by the Poles changed as the battle developed: the Poles were literally fighting for their city street by street. Years later, Sue would meet former *Armia Krajowa* fighters who reflected that she had been helping the RAF in Italy as they were fighting for their city in a common cause.

Over the next months, she would discover new horrors and tragedies, especially in encountering the starving skeletal survivors of the Nazi concentration camps— people who had been rounded up from their homes and taken to the Reich in cattle trucks. As the camps at Belsen, Auschwitz, and elsewhere were liberated by Allied forces, the true scale of the Nazi horror was revealed. People had been sent to the Reich as slave labour, forced to live in filth and squalor, starved and crammed into barracks infested with lice and vermin, with numbers dying daily. In the post-war years, Sue's work for these survivors would dominate her life, and she would be instrumental in offering healing and hope to many.

Meanwhile, there was work to be done, and Sue served with FANY in Italy and in France from 1944 until the final end of the war in 1945. The work involved ferrying supplies and equipment, together with some nursing activities, and general assistance to the military units. This took place against the backdrop of constant tiredness and with limited access to the things that would normally make things easier such as hot food and comfortable sleeping

---

[3]   For an account of the Warsaw Rising and its aftermath, see C. Wolkowinska and J. Bogle, *When the Summer Ended* (Leominster: Gracewing, 1992).

accommodation. Years later, she would remember the things that hallmarked the days—the small cubes of mixed tea-and-milk to which hot water would be added to make a drink, the constant background of dirt and disease, the tragedy but also the friendships and the sense of team-work. Her experiences in these days forged her attitude to things like travel and accommodation: she found she could manage on small quantities of food and in primitive conditions, and for the rest of her life, on any travels, she never sought comfortable hotels and never asked for meals or drinks but simply ate or drank what she was given.

With the declaration of the end of the war in 1945, the FANY's task moved formally from military work to relief work. Sue noted in her memoirs that "the relief units, severally and collectively, were financed by *Amis Volontaires Francais*, (AVF)" and at this stage Sue was still serving with the FANY, one of the units thus financed.

She drove a lorry packed with medical equipment from London to join the ferry to Dieppe where on arrival there was no one to greet her.

> No map was available and petrol was scarce, but I had been given vague directions to go to "the hospital near the Cathedral in Rouen". I reached the ruins of the city in darkness and asked the way from a Frenchman who replied wryly "There once were several hospitals". He directed me to one of the few that had not been destroyed. There, to my relief, I found the other workers (CML 168).

Over the next weeks, Sue was involved in what she had been doing for much of the war—driving heavy vehicles. This time she was carrying medical aid to people living in ruined towns and camping amid broken bits of wall covered with whatever roofing they could find. With no street lighting, signposts or proper landmarks, she learned "how to navigate by smell—the different smells of open sewers, choked drains, decomposing bodies" (CML 169).

The decomposing bodies carried the threat of cholera. Tuberculosis was also beginning to be widespread, along with typhoid—both of these arriving with people returning home from the Nazi concentration camps.

The FANY members slept in a small cubicle in a ruined hospital. In the next room, separated from theirs by a thin partition, was the obstetric unit where women were giving birth: the girls were often woken and asked to help the overworked midwives. The hospital had previously had a large psychiatric unit, and a couple of patients remained, sometimes coming to the girls' window to beg for cigarette ends. On one occasion Sue had to ask for their help as stretcher-bearers when there was a shortage of ambulances.

In addition to ferrying supplies from place to place, Sue helped to run a mobile clinic, working with the French Red Cross. There were queues of people to be inoculated against the various diseases, and also to be disinfected: Sue would later remember "dipping" children like sheep to rid them of infestations of fleas and lice.

The FANY girls' uniforms became worn and filthy—and it was easy to catch lice from the people they were treating. Accommodation was found in all sorts of places, usually with little or no privacy. Their food was rations sent out from Britain, including "dehydrated bananas and powdered milk" which they particularly relished. They were permanently exhausted. It was difficult to wash as water froze overnight in a bucket and soap was small in quantity and of poor quality. Around them were fragments of normal life still continuing—farmers making camembert cheese, nuns in a convent chanting prayers—while the fields and streets still contained broken tanks and old ammunition, and the railway yards still had cattle trucks labelled for use in transporting people to concentration camps. German prisoners were used for clearance work, receiving parcels from the Red Cross and generally having better food than the local French people.

Sue's relief work also took her further afield, to camps where former Allied prisoners-of-war were being held. It was here that she discovered one of the most tragic and sickening events of the war: the forced deportation to the USSR of Russians who had fought alongside the Allies but who were now being sent back to Russia to certain imprisonment and death in the gulag.[4] The vicious brutality of Stalin's rule in the USSR was known: the 1930s had seen millions of people die in the great chain of labour camps established in the Arctic Circle, in the forced starvation famines of the Russian countryside, and in the purges of whole classes of people including peasant farmers.

The Russian prisoners-of-war in 1945 were victims of the agreements made at the Yalta conference where Churchill, Stalin, and the USA's President Roosevelt met to discuss the future of Europe. Stalin insisted that all Soviet prisoners be returned to the USSR. No one really trusted him, and the grim fate of the prisoners was certain. But it seems that little effort was made to find ways of avoiding the cruel—and dishonest—deportation of these men against their will. Sue was to discover the situation at first hand, and was determined to do what she could for at least a small number of the prisoners.

> In 1945 these Soviet prisoners pleaded to have the
> opportunity to enjoy a new life in another country

---

4   For the full story, see N. Bethell, *The Last Secret* (London: Andrew Deutsch, 1974), and N. Tolstoy, *Victims of Yalta* (London: Hodder and Stoughton, 1977). A London monument to the victims was dedicated in 1982 but repeatedly vandalised: a fresh one was dedicated in 1988 and stands in a garden in Thurlow Place Gardens, London SW7.

> removed from the past. Thousands of them had
> already experienced the worst years of Communist
> rule in the Soviet Union, including famine and
> Stalin's reign of terror and they were terrified of
> what awaited them if they returned... (CML 154).

She remembered "scenes of tragedy and sheer horror" in the hospitals and camps as the decision was implemented. The Soviet authorities understood that because these men had seen something of life in the West and knew how much better it was in every way than life under Communism, they would be a danger to the Soviet system by telling the truth to their families or neighbours. No mercy would be shown to them.

Sue now took action on her own initiative. After many of the prisoners pleaded with her, she worked with a Russian social worker, Ludmilla,[5] to protect and hide as many of them as she could, providing forged papers and taking groups, hidden in ambulances, to other camps where they could claim to belong to other nationalities.

This was dangerous work, and completely beyond anything she was allowed to do as a relief worker and still officially a member of the British Forces. Sue was working against the authorities of her own country: taking her ambulance by roundabout routes to avoid the checkpoints established by Britain's Royal Military Police, arranging forged papers, and organising deception in the full knowledge of what she was doing. She never had any regrets about this: she had to watch while large crowds of men that she was unable to save were herded on to trains. She also had the ghastly experience of entering a dark hut where men went to wash, and finding several bodies hanging there—

---

[5]   Sue Ryder adds that it was also necessary to help Ludmilla, who
        similarly faced repatriation: she went into hiding and was able to
        emigrate to the USA (CML 155).

Russian prisoners who had taken their own lives rather than face lingering death in the concentration camps of the Arctic Circle. She never forgot this sight. A Russian Orthodox priest came in to bless the limp bodies (CML 155).

Half a century later, her sorrow and indignation would ring out from the pages of her autobiography as she wrote about the thousands of men sent by ship or cattle-wagons to long years of misery and lingering death in the Soviet gulag, and the horror of the British soldiers ordered to force them on to the trains.

Sue had never been frightened of taking initiatives when the need arose. She was proud to serve in the First Aid Nursing Yeomanry but the commitment to Christian service could not stop there. Perhaps, whether she realised it or not, the repatriation of the Soviet prisoners, together with the recognition that the courageous Polish agents with whom she had served in SOE would not now see their country liberated from tyranny, marked something of a turning-point. When the need arose, she would sometimes simply have to work on her own.

4 THE BOYS

IT WAS IN France in 1945 that Sue first discovered the plight of the young prisoners she came to call "The Boys". These were young men, mostly Polish, who had recently been freed from various Nazi concentration camps and, trying to reach home and find their families, had nowhere to live and were starving. Many had resorted to theft and violence in order to survive, and had been arrested by the Allied military authorities and imprisoned. They had little, if any, access to any legal advice or help, and were at a disadvantage because of their lack of language skills. Their wretched position as homeless, stateless and starving seemed not to be recognised, and they were simply treated as criminals under standard pre-war laws.

Beginning in France, Sue's work in visiting these young men in prison soon spread to Germany. She saw the project as a simple extension of her relief work, although much of it seems to have been a more or less private initiative, and it continued for some years after she had left the FANY and the service of the AVF.

It is not clear how Sue managed to become an independent relief worker, without any formal structure or organisation to back her up, and with no official status. She herself described it as a natural progression from all that had gone before:

> After I had for some years worked with and for international relief units in Europe, they withdrew—the Red Cross in 1949, because of heavy commitments elsewhere, and the Guide Interna-

tional Service[1] in 1951, when they had exhausted
their funds. I continued the work on my own. It
never occurred to me to give up. Everything in my
childhood, and my experiences during the War,
seemed to lead to this inevitable decision. Those
were very difficult days, with no funds and no
certainty of any support. I shared the frugal life of
those who faced uncertainty, sickness and disap-
pointment most of the time, and they told me they
felt I was one of them (CML 225).

Asked about this many years later, she explained "I felt
very strongly that I was single, I was free—I didn't have
any money but I felt very strongly that somehow God
meant me to stay there, so I did"[2].

Discovering the plight of The Boys, Sue began to help
them, and thus began a connection that would last for
decades. In these first weeks, she worked amid the chaos
of the immediate post-war period when Germany was—as
it would remain for some years—a country under the
military control of the Allied forces.[3] This meant that
ultimate decisions were made by the local Allied Com-

---

[1] The Guide International Service was established by the Girl
Guides Association in 1942 with the aim of sending Guides into
Europe to carry out relief work when the war ended.

[2] Sue Ryder, speaking to Michael Parkinson on *Desert Island Discs*,
BBC Radio 4, January 1987

[3] Winston Churchill announced the principle of Unconditional
Surrender in January 1945. On June 5th 1945, following VE Day
and the end of the war in Europe, the governments of the United
Kingdom, the USA, the USSR and the provisional government
of the French Republic announced four zones of occupation in
Germany: "an eastern zone to the USSR, a north-western zone
to the United Kingdom, a south-western zone to the USA, a
western zone to France". See *Documents on Germany under
Occupation 1945–54*, (London: Oxford University Press 1955).

mander, which in principle meant that Sue could contact
the British, American or French authorities.

*Sue Ryder's work with relief agencies after the end of the Second
World War, was partially funded by the Guide International
Service, which meant that she exchanged her First Aid Nursing
Yeomanry uniform for that of a Girl Guide leader*

The Allied military authorities were chiefly concerned
with keeping order, and trying to ensure that some form
of transport and delivery of basic supplies such as food
was maintained. There was widespread hunger, homeless-
ness, and lack of basic medical care. Many people in the

bombed-out cities slept in cellars or old air-raid bunkers. Thousands of men were still missing—many women would never discover the fate of their soldier-husbands, caught up in the bitter fighting on the eastern front.[4]

The new Federal Republic was created in 1949 but before that time the Western Allies gradually handed over various administrative tasks to local Germans.[5] The Allied authorities sought to insist that any German holding any form of public office had to produce evidence that he was not a Nazi. For this purpose a series of passes were issued, for officials at various levels, indicating that the holder was "clean".[6] But bureaucratic attitudes among prison officials, whatever the official's political views, often caused problems for Sue when she tried to help young prisoners.

At the start it was essentially a matter of seeking justice for young men who had been accused of crimes but who were really war victims who were struggling to stay alive, and finding food and shelter where they could.

"In my experience, the lawless behaviour of the Boys could nearly always be attributed to the atrocious conditions during the War and the chaos of its aftermath. Hunger was a prime factor. There were many who raided local farms for food and clothing. They usually operated in small groups, and sometimes—although this was not always intended—shooting occurred" (CML 178).

---

[4]   German soldiers captured by the Soviets were taken to harsh prison-camps beyond the Arctic Circle: many died there, and the final remnants were only able to return to Germany after prolonged negotiations by the first Chancellor of the newly-created Federal Republic of Germany, Konrad Adenauer, ten years after the war ended.

[5]   The Eastern (Soviet) zone of Germany became a Communist dominated "democratic republic" in 1949. Sue's work was in the western zones of Germany.

[6]   Such a pass came to be known as a "Persilschein" after the popular America/British soap powder.

A major problem, as Sue would later recall, was that the Boys were in prisons where many of the staff imposed a system of rigid rules and punishments which did not allow for any alteration regardless of the circumstances.

Sue worked carefully and systematically, with a file for each prisoner, using a ring-binder and later boxes of material. She had to make use of her knowledge of German, and to familiarise herself with the often complex legal position of each case. It was not easy to obtain access to all the papers she needed to establish the full facts, and there were no photocopying facilities.

The stories of the Boys were heart-rending. One, a former member of the Polish Resistance who had survived Auschwitz/Birkenau and Sachsenhausen, weighed six stone when liberated by the American Army. After a spell in hospital, he lived rough and tried to earn by selling scrap metal, which at that time was unlawful. He was sentenced by an Allied Military Court to three years in prison. His sentence was eventually commuted but he was stateless and without papers, starving and homeless.

> Little wonder that he had reached desperation point and wept when he came to my office in Neustadt. While queues of other distracted and distraught people waited outside, messages for help kept coming in from block leaders and also from others at the hospital. There were never enough hours to try and cope (CML188).

Later the Allied courts handed over jurisdiction to the German authorities. This made for even greater difficulties. A prisoner was officially allowed to be represented by a lawyer but these were "often of no assistance or showed no interest in the case. There were lawyers too who would only take the case if they were promised payment for their services" (CML 177).

Many of the Boys had suffered so badly that they were mentally unstable, and little allowance was made for this. Visiting as many as thirty prisoners in a day, and struggling to keep up with all the necessary paperwork, Sue had to work systematically, and also to use tact and perseverance with officialdom. She would later recall her exasperation at some of the German officials, who seemed not to understand the plight of the prisoners or who were openly contemptuous of them. While some, as the years of her work continued, would be helpful and treated her with courtesy, others insisted on, for example, opening up every small gift that she brought—slicing through fruit on the grounds that it might contain a note, and banning nuts for the same reason.

The various prisons and hospitals were spread over a wide area of devastated Germany, and it was almost impossible to find anywhere to stay so Sue mostly slept and worked in her lorry. Food was also extremely difficult to obtain and she would later recall often feeling faint due to lack of nourishment. There was a lack of humanity at many levels, especially in the early years. Sue would later recall:

> Owing to the number of Boys in some of the prisons, and the problems and time it took to deal with them—often from 7.30am until 6pm—I was obliged to remain in the prison all day on my visits. I was rarely offered food, or even the use of a loo. More than once when I asked for the latter I was told by the warders that they had no place for a woman! ... Before the appointment of social workers in Bavaria the prison chaplains were supposed to be responsible for the welfare of the prisoners. Some of these chaplains and, indeed, all the warders and Directors for many years after the War ended, still referred to the prisoners by

> number, and I was constantly scolded for referring
> to them by their names … (CML 202)

Capital punishment was imposed where the homeless, stateless youths had resorted to violence in their hunger, and Sue spent much time pleading for their lives to be spared, although sometimes the alternative of lifelong imprisonment seemed almost more cruel. One young man, who had been fourteen when taken by the Nazis for slave labour and ended in the concentration camp at Belsen, had weighed just four stone when liberated by the British. Roaming with others, starving and with no possibility of finding his old home again, he joined an attack on a former SS man, and was brought before an Allied Military Court and sentenced to be shot. Sue had tried to help and a lawyer pleaded his case: "He referred again to the boy's bearing throughout the trial, his candour, honesty, and his readiness to put no obstacle in the way of preliminary investigations. Few, on this evidence, it seemed, could doubt the boy's real potential for good."[7] It was to no avail: he was in due course shot by a British firing squad.

There were other similar cases, and Sue Ryder kept and later publicised the moving letter handed to her written by an 18-year-old who wrote it on a scrap of paper:

> I am leaving this letter with my companion, for you
> to remember us. Please if you get the chance have
> the courage to read this letter to our friends. May
> I ask you to try and find my father, who as you
> know has been missing since the Gestapo took him,
> and give him a copy, too. I implore you not to let
> this letter out of your hands, and to say goodbye to
> everyone…We are taking leave of you for ever and

---

[7]   A. J. Forrest, *But some there be: The story of the Forgotten Allies and of Sue Ryder's relief work* (London, Robert Hale Ltd, 1957), p. 56.

our beloved country. Let us hope that somewhere
there will be understanding for what we have done
at this early age and in exile. We must die at the
hands of our Allies for shooting the SS who killed
all our families. We fought in the same cause, but
this and the things which followed are all forgotten.
We are leaving this world after receiving extreme
unction from Father G.[8]

In cases where she was able to obtain the release of a Boy,
there was the question of where he might live. Most had
no possibility of returning home—their families were dead
or missing in Siberia, and their town or village destroyed
in the war. Some were eventually able to emigrate to
Australia or the USA and make new lives—others were
able to find work in Britain or in Germany. Sue established
hostels for some in various German towns—these offered
rudimentary accommodation but were better than the
former air-raid bunkers or cellars of ruined buildings
where many homeless still slept, at constant risk of theft,
drunken arguments, fights, and rats. The recently founded
Oxford Committee for Famine Relief—later famous as
Oxfam for relief work across the world—helped to fund
these hostels. In 1955 Sue established one at Hessen and
made a tiny office for herself there with a camp bed and a
table for her typewriter. She created an organisation
dedicated to St Christopher to raise funds and organise
the running of the project. Many of the "Boys" who were

---

[8]   Forrest, *But some there be,* pp. 56–57. "Extreme Unction" refers
to the sacrament of the anointing of the sick, in the nomenclature
for the sacrament in the West from the late twelfth century until
1972. It is unlikely that this anointing would have been adminis-
tered to those in danger of dying through war, general absolution
would seem the sacrament of choice. Different would be the case
of a soldier who was already wounded, who would then receive
the anointing of the sick.

able make new lives for themselves because of her help, retained links with Sue for years, and their stories became interwoven, as we will see, with her subsequent work following the establishment of her Living Memorial.

Long years later a British newspaper account of Sue's work with The Boys told the story:

> She alone remembered the "jail birds"—boys, Russian or Polish especially, released from the camps in 1945, their families dead, homes destroyed, flung into grim post-war Germany to live on their wits. Some stole, others took vengeance, when chance came, on SS men. Many were executed by British and American courts; others were given life sentences in German prisons.
>
> For lesser criminals, no provision was made for education, rehabilitation, help to employment on release, or even citizenship. Like so many, they landed on Ryder's lap. In 1955 she had founded the St Christopher Kreis to aid them, and the St Christopher Settlement in Hanover, where they could be received and helped on release.
>
> She got a little help from a few Germans—notably in Hesse—and from the German Red Cross, but, generally, met obstruction from authority. She drove regularly to visit, in different prisons, men, now grown up, who had not seen a woman for years until she came and fought for them, appeared in court for them, and sought amnesties or jobs overseas.[9]

Sue struggled with immigration authorities in Australia and the USA to get some of her Boys, and other Displaced People, as they were known, into those countries. There were stringent—and, in retrospect, rather cruel—health

---

[9]   *The Guardian*, 3 November 2000.

regulations. Inevitably, people who had been in Auschwitz
and Belsen and similar camps had TB and other diseases,
and American and Australian rules banned their entry to
those countries. There were some heartbreaking decisions
made because of this, with families separated, children
being allowed to leave and their parents being told they
must remain in the grim camps in which they were trying
to live. In the case of the Boys, a prison record naturally
made for great difficulties.

A young woman, slight of build and often exhausted,
Sue must have made an odd figure as she battled with
prison authorities. But she was a woman with a very strong
sense of dedication, and took on battles with British,
American, and German authorities with patience and skill.
She learned that the most effective way was to stand her
ground, and patiently follow all the regulations, insisting
on seeing these in print, and on contacting the relevant
higher authority when possible.

> German prison officials time and again expressed
> their amazement at this blue-eyed, slight, fair-
> haired and attractive young Englishwoman who
> had pressed the bells outside their prison entrances
> and handed them lists, drawn up by the Penal
> Branch, of "jail birds" she must see. As she went to
> each in his cell, her quick mind, ready laugh and
> natural sympathy banished any suspicion a much-
> embittered man might have harboured of an inter-
> fering foreigner.[10]

In 1949 the Allied authorities declared an amnesty for the
majority of Displaced Persons for crimes committed
between 1945 and 1947. This did not mean an end to the
problems, but at least it offered some hope for many and also
opened up new possibilities for Sue to bring help and relief.

---

[10]   Forrest, *But some there be*, p. 58.

Meanwhile, she was also busy planning something more permanent, and this would begin when she returned home to Britain in 1951.

5 BACK HOME

S UE DID NOT have a permanent home while working with prisoners and Displaced People in the years immediately after the war. In fact, her status and income during those years has something of a mystery about it. After leaving the FANY, she worked for various relief services, and these would have provided a salary, but after a while ceased. At a practical level, how did she live, and how did she fund her activities?

The simple answer is that she received help and donations from various people—especially her mother to whom she had always been close. This funding then developed into a formal structure, and she later described this in her autobiography. "The work I was doing in the prisons and hospitals of Europe grew so quickly that by the time I returned to England on short leave in 1951–2, I had decided that it was necessary to form a small committee and to register the Living Memorial with the Charity Commissioners. After discussing the germ of the idea with people I knew, and in particular with my mother, the Sue Ryder Foundation as it is today was born" (CML 225). Her next step was to find a house where she could welcome the people she intended to help: displaced people permanently disabled from the effects of their experiences in Nazi concentration camps, who could be offered a home and the chance of a new life in Britain. She needed somewhere large, ideally in a peaceful rural area, with some land attached so that people could enjoy some outdoor life and gardens could be created—and it had to be a building that was attractive and would feel like a real home.

In post-war Britain, there were many great houses whose owners could not only no longer afford to live in them, but were also struggling to find any purchasers or any institutions that might be interested. Huge properties which a few decades earlier had been filled with family, staff and guests were now effectively redundant. In a country where food was rationed and fuel in winter hard to find, where whole streets had been destroyed by bombs and people made homeless, there was little interest in the plight of large, fine, decaying buildings belonging to families who could not afford their upkeep or the staff to run them. Sue Ryder's own background gave her knowledge and understanding of the potential of such buildings and she started to seek them out, with the idea that one of these could be suitable for her great project.

Sadly, she was unable to raise the necessary funds—although later on, she did play her part in rescuing some old houses which would prove to be ideal as Sue Ryder Homes. But the early 1950s were not a good time for such a project and years later, her regret still rings through her comment in her autobiography: "It is sad to relate, but it is true, and perhaps not well known by the public, that 712 country houses in Britain were demolished, gutted or fell into ruin between the years 1945 and 1975" (CML 226).

Eventually, it was clear that she would have to offer her mother's home, the Old Rectory at Cavendish in Suffolk, a Tudor farmhouse where Mabel Ryder had been living since her widowhood. It had a long history, interwoven with that of the village. From the start, Sue's mother had been warmly supportive of all that Sue was doing, and the two were united in a commitment to taking the work forward. It was arranged that a small family flat would be retained in the house —where Sue's mother lived for a while before moving to a cottage nearby—and the rest would be entirely given over to a residential home for concentration camp victims, and others in need.

The funds that Sue had been raising, together with her own legacy from her father, and a bank loan, were sufficient to enable a start to be made on the necessary renovations. Professional help was sought and workmen moved in—but much work was also done by volunteers, in what was to become a major theme in the decades-long story of the Sue Ryder Foundation. In her autobiography she described with relish how old dark green paint and layers of wallpaper were removed, using a blow-lamp, wire brushes and sandpaper, and how people sang as they worked, and gathered together for much-needed cups of tea at the end of each day (CML 231).

In due course extensions were added to the house, with the removal of a greenhouse and its replacement by an extra wing. To comply with standards required by the health authorities—though these were far less demanding then than now—extra bathrooms were created. As a first priority, a chapel was established and Mass celebrated regularly. This was a pattern that would be followed in all Sue Ryder Homes over the next years. At Cavendish in the first years there was a resident priest, and visiting holiday groups from Poland usually included a priest too. If for some reason the resident priest was away, one would come from nearby Clare Priory.[1] The chapel was created from what had been a boxroom and adjoining shed, and all its furnishings were donated—the altar from a supporter in Cornwall, oak pews from a boys' home in Peterborough, the holy water stoop from religious sisters in what was then Yugoslavia.

---

[1]   Clare Priory was established in 1248, closed under Henry VIII in 1538, and sold to various owners over the next years. Its final owner Lady Mary Barker made it available on generous terms to the Augustinian Friars in 1953. It is now the centre of a busy parish and also offers retreats and conferences.

From the start, there were generous gifts of furniture, household goods, and kitchen equipment. There were also large numbers of visitors because Cavendish still, at that time, had a railway station[2] and Sue's work was becoming increasingly known. Strong links were established with the local Anglican church, St Mary the Virgin, which stands across the village green from the house. Clergy from the church came to the house each week to celebrate the Eucharist, and residents and visitors were also encouraged to visit the church. Successive clergy and parishioners would take an active interest in Sue's work over the years, providing much voluntary support, practical work and fund-raising.

While all this was happening, Sue was deeply involved in a major project which was to become central to her work over the next years—offering holidays to displaced people to give them a break from their grim surroundings in their temporary accommodation in Germany, and to establish links for them in other parts of Europe.

By the 1950s, the immediate chaos of post-war Europe had given way to a more organised structure of national boundaries, passports, and visas. Sue had become used to the weariness of waiting for documents to be checked and paperwork sorted. But she was not averse to making her own arrangements where necessary. The teenager who had hidden Russian prisoners-of-war in her truck to prevent them being returned to the Soviet Union was more than capable of fitting extra Displaced People into an already overcrowded vehicle and whisking them through frontiers.

Sue liked traditions and cheery nicknames—it was all part of the Sue Ryder style. Her cars—and, later, her lorries

---

2   The station, opened in the 1860s, was closed in 1967 as part of the "Beeching Cuts", the unpopular—and from today's perspective badly mistaken—decision by Richard Beeching, chairman of the British Railways Board, to close down large parts of Britain's railway network.

and buses—all had names. In "Alice" she travelled around post-war Germany visiting prisons and refugee camps. Later she acquired "Maybug", so named because of its make, a Triumph Mayflower, and "Jeremiah" a bus which would take her on innumerable journeys.

Taking a large number of people from various refugee camps across Germany to Denmark required, however, a good-sized means of transport, and Sue drove a special bus created by a Latvian refugee out of materials found in scrap-heaps and junk-yards. Together with another couple of buses it formed a convoy which took a group across the Danish frontier for what became the first of many summer holidays that brought health and new hope to people who for years had known nothing but ill-health and bleak conditions.

In typical style this trip had its nickname, "Operation Drainpipe". But the organisation, involving Danish hospitals and clinics, families and welfare centres, was anything but simple, as it required the sorting out of a large number of small details from language problems to specific health requirements. It would prove, however, to be the launch of a popular scheme which tapped into local generosity and brought not only joy to the refugees but welcome publicity, funds and assistance for the organisers. Over the next years, it acquired a life of its own, and friendships were forged with host families which lasted for years and stretched across to new generations. Years later, Sue would recall the warmth of the welcome in Denmark as she arrived with a busload of tired travellers from the Displaced People's camps, and the delicious coffee, rolls, butter and ham that greeted them—luxuries unknown in Germany's refugee camps at that time, and also in Britain where wartime food rationing was still in place.

The Danish holiday scheme worked well, but it was clear that in the longer term, it would make more sense for the holidays to take place in England. In Denmark, hospitality was given by Danish families, but it was clearly easier to keep the group together and have them all stay in one place. Thus the decision was made to bring the groups to Suffolk, and for this purpose Sue's mother, who had formed a committee to help organise the project, looked at possible places where they could stay. A solution was found at Melford Hall,[3] in nearby Long Melford. It was an ancient house with monastic origins dating back to before the Norman Conquest. Part of the building, dating from Tudor times, had been badly damaged by a fire in 1942, but restoration had been carried out and one wing was available, and a lease was arranged to the Forgotten Allies Trust, the name Sue had given to this first part of her Living Memorial.

Mabel Ryder worked to furnish the rooms, using her Edwardian sense of country house hospitality to make them attractive and welcoming, with fresh flowers and attractive wall-hangings. As with the Old Rectory at Cavendish, furniture and other necessities were donated, along with funds and volunteer help. It was not possible to buy the building but throughout the 1950s it became, in effect, an extension of Cavendish—they were only a short journey apart—and the base for the holiday visitors from where they were taken on trips and outings during their stay. Thus in 1959 the Holiday Scheme formally came into being.

In addition to bringing adults to Britain for holidays, Sue worked closely with the Ockenden Venture founded by Joyce Pearce,[4] which offered homes and educational

---

[3]   The monastic buildings, owned by the monks of Bury St Edmunds, were closed under Henry VIII and the house later passed to the Cordell and Savage families. In the 18th century it was sold to the Parker family and its last owner, Ulla, Lady Hyde Parker, passed it to the care of the National Trust in 1960. It is currently open to the public.

opportunities in Britain for refugee children. Sue's involvement included ferrying the children across Europe in "Jeremiah". By now, her work was becoming well known. The Archbishop in Belgium arranged that she could stop at any convent or monastery along the route and find a warm welcome with coffee and a hot cooked breakfast and there were even cafes and restaurants along the route, too, that offered food and hot drinks for the long night rides.

As the holiday scheme got under way and became known, it attracted widespread support. In Britain, Rotary Clubs organised trips and activities for the holidaymakers, taking them to Windsor, Runnymede, the Tower of London, the Chelsea Flower Show, and elsewhere, and Sir William "Billy" Butlin offered free accommodation for groups at his holiday camp at Clacton.

As soon as the house at Cavendish was ready—in 1953—Sue was able to offer a permanent home to those whose sufferings in the concentration camps had left them permanently disabled and unable to care for themselves. Sue's plan was they could be given a home and chance of a new life "and even do a little light work, and feel really useful, and human beings again". She estimated that there were some 220,000 displaced people in Europe still living in squalid conditions, including survivors of Buchenwald, Ravensbruck, and other Nazi concentration camps, many of them suffering from TB and other serious illnesses.

---

[4] The Ockenden Venture was established by Joyce Pearce and two friends in 1951, and took its name from Ockenden, the Pearce family home in Woking, Surrey. Initially established to help child refugees from Eastern Europe, it went on to care for Vietnamese children in the 1980s. It is now known as Ockenden International and runs various educational and other welfare projects in Sudan, Pakistan, and Uganda among other places.

Sue Ryder after receiving her OBE at Buckingham Palace in 1957.
She is accompanied by one of her volunteer staff, Sister Maria.

She explained in a television interview that these people "were enslaved and deported by the Nazis. They are very anti-Communist and that's why they didn't want to go back behind the Iron Curtain".[5] Her plan was to offer a home where they would not only receive care but feel they belonged, and had a purpose in life.

The theme of "Forgotten Allies" struck a chord with people in Britain: there was an awareness that Poland and other countries had suffered during the war but had not gained freedom, and that there was in a sense a debt of honour to be repaid. Gifts poured into Cavendish, and newspapers and magazines reported the stories of the concentration camp survivors who were finding peace, security and good medical care in this comfortable old house in the English countryside.

In October 1957—still only in her early 30s—Sue Ryder was awarded the OBE, the Order of the British Empire, for her work with the Forgotten Allies Friendship Scheme.

---

[5]   "Stories behind *This is your life*" June 1957.

6 INTO HER STRIDE

From the mid-1950s onwards, the story of Sue Ryder's life is the story of the expansion of her work: establishing more Sue Ryder Homes, caring for a wider range of people and looking overseas.

Her own personal story also developed, but she wrote and spoke very little about the deepest parts of her life—her religious faith and her family. What she did affirm, publicly and with evident sincerity, was a strong affection for her parents and gratitude towards them, together with a straightforward orthodox Christian faith which she practised in a fervent but traditional way without exaggerated signals of piety. It was her stronghold.

In childhood, she had been taken to Walsingham where the Rector, the Rev Alfred Hope Patten, was a family friend. He had re-established the ancient shrine of Our Lady of Walsingham which had been destroyed at the Reformation. The theology and forms of worship, focusing on the Eucharist and on Marian devotion, were Anglo-Catholic in style and shaped Sue's spiritual life.

When Sue's work with SOE during World War II brought her into contact with Poles, she would have found their Roman Catholic beliefs and practices very familiar. At some point—the date is uncertain—she joined the Roman Catholic Church. She would remain a dedicated and enthusiastic Catholic for the rest of her life.

The work of her Foundation always had an ecumenical base, and all major events involved both Anglican and Catholic clergy. Sue's mother remained a committed

Anglican, active with the Mothers' Union and teaching in the local Sunday school.

At Cavendish, when work was being carried out to create the first Sue Ryder Home, the first priority had been the chapel. This would be the pattern for all the Homes over the next years. "Where will the chapel be?" was always the first question asked when looking at a property that might be suitable. Sue attended Mass daily whenever possible. She spoke about her faith with simple honesty: she was an unashamed, fully committed Christian and this was the key to her work, her world-view and the direction of her life. Her childhood faith had matured with her, and was nourished by the example of courageous Christians that she met over the years, and by her steadfast commitment to prayer and to regular worship.

Sue was now doing something that few other people in the West were doing at that time: she was travelling to Poland. This was a time when contact beyond the Iron Curtain was rare and difficult. It is unclear from her autobiography how Sue managed the complicated permissions and paperwork. What is certain is that, among the large community of exiled Poles in Britain, her actions were regarded with some suspicion. The Communist government in Poland was held in power by the USSR and the threat of the Red Army. It had gained power through the circumstances of war—Churchill and Roosevelt were powerless to take any effective action against Stalin's landgrab when meeting at Potsdam and at Yalta to draw the post-war map of Europe. Anyone willingly travelling to Poland at the height of the Cold War might well be assumed to have Communist sympathies—that was certainly the feeling held by many Poles in London, including former Armia Krajowa soldiers, Battle of Britain pilots, and veterans of the Soviet camps and of the bitter fighting at Monte Cassino and elsewhere.

Sue's motives were purely humanitarian. She went to Poland—always driving herself, never flying or using trains—to the ruins of Warsaw to help with rebuilding projects and to bring necessities to people who were desperately poor and in need.

"She really did give herself wholeheartedly to Poland" Mrs Halina Kent would later recall "She certainly didn't support Communism—on the contrary. All that mattered to her was helping the suffering. She was giving help when no one else could or would.

> It's important to understand that, under Communism, it was impossible to do anything except under that system. None of the homes she established in Poland were under her name—they were never her property and never had the Sue Ryder sign on them. What would happen was that the authorities provided the land and she would bring in all the equipment, all the materials, everything that was needed, from Britain. In the end she had the Communist authorities eating out of her hand.
>
> But it was only after the fall of Communism that plaques went up in the institutions she had founded and she was publicly acknowledged. Long before that, however, Polish people knew—they knew all about her, and they knew what the country owed to her.[1]

Sue's first attempts to bring aid were in the ruins of Warsaw: some ninety per cent of all the buildings had been destroyed: homes, hospitals, schools, shops, churches,

---

[1] Conversation with author, November 2020. Halina Kent worked for Sue Ryder from 1990, establishing the Foundation in Poland after the fall of Communism: her story is told later in this book.

railway stations. The railway lines were not working, and there was no means of contacting the rest of the country as no one owned a car, and there was no petrol. There was a great will to survive and to rebuild the city: Sue would later recall seeing "Warsaw lives" scrawled in the dust on her lorry (CML 378). She saw at first hand the attempts of people to survive, and later the clearing of land-mines and unexploded bombs, and the beginning, in 1947–48, of plans for blocks of flats.

Her first major project was the establishment of a home for badly disabled girls and women in a former health resort at Konstancin, some miles out of the city. Most had been trapped at home, unable to attend school because they could not walk, and lacking any medical care. The main disease was severe rheumatoid arthritis, and many of the patients were suffering acute pain. The Home was eventually opened in 1957. Over the next years, many of the young women would be helped and enabled to go on to have careers and families. Others would live permanently at the Home and lead busy and happy lives there: they completed their education and passed examinations and took degrees in mathematics or economics, they ran the house together taking charge of meals and entertainments, some taking jobs and travelling regularly to work. Over the years additions and developments at the home would enable independent flats to be created for long-term residents, and other initiatives included the creation of a co-operative through which residents made and sold dolls in traditional Polish costume.

While travelling regularly to Poland, negotiating with builders and suppliers, transporting materials from docks, and working with the authorities on plans and projects, Sue was also still extremely busy in Britain with the holiday schemes for concentration camp victims and for more permanent care for some of them.

She was becoming better known. Her emphasis on the theme of "forgotten allies" and on the relief of suffering as a way of commemorating those who had died in the War, resonated deeply with people, and funds were coming in. Cavendish was now well established and there were plans for more Homes, and more help for the victims of the Nazis and for the disabled and elderly. Her Sue Ryder Foundation with its message of a "Living Memorial" was becoming part of British life.

One evening in September 1956, Sue went to the King's Theatre at Hammersmith in West London for what she thought would be a short broadcast talk. Television was something new and exciting at that time, and families across Britain were buying TV sets, or visiting friends or relations to watch favourite weekly programmes. One such programme was "This is your life" presented by a popular broadcaster, Eamonn Andrews. The key was to find people who played some active role in public life, and to spring a surprise: lured to the studio on some pretext, they would find Andrews announcing, before TV cameras: "This is your life!" and holding out a large red book listing all the significant dates and achievements from over the years. Friends and work colleagues would then arrive, one by one, on to the stage, so that the person's life would be celebrated and the story told. It made extremely popular viewing, and had become something of a national institution.

Sue Ryder was, by all accounts, actually confused and annoyed when she found herself thus accosted. She did not watch television and knew nothing about the show. Central to the show's popularity was that the "victim" was genuinely surprised—family and friends who would appear were pledged to secrecy.

*The TV programme "This is Your Life" in 1956 brought
nationwide fame*

"I thought it was quite extraordinary—a bit dotty
really"[2] she confessed thirty years later, discussing the
experience on a radio show with Michael Parkinson. She
had, she said, heard of television but had not got around
to watching any, so the whole concept of the show was
foreign to her. Only when she saw her mother, who was
among the various friends and colleagues who had gathered, did she feel slightly reassured. Those involved
included Polish people she had helped, including several
with powerful and dramatic background stories, and also
Joyce Pearce of the Ockenden Venture and other supporters. The programme turned out to be a huge success,
bringing nationwide publicity and in turn many donations
for her work.

---

[2]   Sue Ryder, speaking with Michael Parkinson on *Desert Island
Discs*, January 1987.

It was broadcast in November 1956 and a year later Eamonn Andrews interviewed her again to discuss how it had gone: "You were fairly cross" he told her, and she confessed that she was "still annoyed" with her committee for having set the whole project in motion[3]. But she was grateful for the publicity and touched by the many donations that arrived—she kept some of the letters and quoted them in her autobiography many years later. At the end of the discussion with Eamonn Andrews he noted that she spent much time travelling to Europe to help people in the camps, and asked when she would be off again. In typical style she said she was actually leaving "as soon as possible after this, in my little car", which would be crammed with things that people needed.

---

[3]   "Stories behind *This is your life*" June 1957.

7 LEONARD CHESHIRE

ORMER ROYAL AIR Force bomber pilot Group
Captain Leonard Cheshire VC had captured the
public imagination. In addition to gaining the Victoria Cross, Britain's highest award for bravery, he held
the DSO and the DFC, and was one of the most highly
decorated RAF pilots of the Second World War. In the
post-war years he had founded a whole network of Homes
offering care for the terminally ill and the disabled.

A convert to the Roman Catholic faith, Cheshire had
also become known as a writer and commentator. At the
point at which he met Sue Ryder, he was a national figure,
and Sue must have been one of the few people in Britain
who was unfamiliar with his name. Busy driving back and
forth across Europe, organising care for refugees, tackling
the large amounts of paperwork involved in acquiring and
administering the Homes she was establishing, Sue had
little time for watching television or reading the newspapers. Cheshire, for his part, had not heard of Sue either.
He was busy with Ampthill House, the stately home in
Bedfordshire, dating back to the 14th century, which he
hoped to turn into a Cheshire Home, and also with plans
for a home for sufferers with tuberculosis. He was organising weekend pilgrimages to Lourdes in France, wrote
regularly for the *Catholic Herald* among several other
publications, and had mapped out a number of other old
houses which might prove usable as Cheshire Homes.

The suggestion that Ryder and Cheshire should meet
had come from a mutual friend, who felt that Sue would

be interested to see Ampthill.[1] Sue drove there from Cavendish. She was not one to be deterred by the fact that the main gate was locked—she found her way in by a side entrance and encountered Cheshire in the kitchen.

Sue habitually ate and drank frugally—after the car journey from Suffolk to Bedfordshire on a winter afternoon she politely declined the offer of a cup of tea but the conversation flourished. The pair had so much in common centred on a shared faith, a deep understanding of the impact and significance of the War and its aftermath, a commitment to care for suffering people, and considerable competence and expertise acquired as a result of personal experience. They talked about practicalities. Sue was interested in Cheshire's plans for Ampthill and the ways in which he planned to accomplish them. Later, neither spoke about this first encounter as being "love at first sight" or even as having made an immediate impact. It was an undramatic start to what was to become one of the 20th century's most famous partnerships. Cheshire's main memory later was that Sue seemed rather tired [2]– as well she might, as she had only recently returned from one of her long cross-Europe journeys and had been busy with administrative work every moment since.

---

[1]   Ampthill House has links with, among others, Catherine of Aragon who was sent there by Henry VIII when he wanted to dissolve his marriage. The present building dates from the 17th century. During World War II it was used by the Army. It became a Cheshire Home in 1955 and in the 1970s the Cheshire Foundation moved out to new premises in Bedford. Ampthill is now divided into several luxury apartments. A recent advertisement for one of them notes the house as the place where Sue Ryder and Cheshire met.

[2]   For an account of the meeting, see R. Morris, *Cheshire: The Biography of Leonard Cheshire VC OM* (London, Penguin 2001), p. 314

But if there was not immediate romance, there was certainly interest and they agreed to meet again.

And there was India. Cheshire had been active there for some while and was keen to extend his work, especially for people suffering from leprosy, and for handicapped children and young people who were unable to get an education or find work. It would not just be a single Home but a whole community, with family houses and a school and more. He had received the support of Jawaharlal Nehru, who had become the first Prime Minister of independent India. Nehru was moved and impressed on meeting Cheshire and learning of his plans, and his public support and encouragement helped to push the project forward.

In the summer of 1958 Cheshire and Sue—who had stayed in touch and corresponded—met in Poland at one of Sue's projects. By now they were discussing some joint ventures, especially in India. By the latter part of the year they were looking seriously at the common future of their work. As they had each been running an organisation for some years—and each organisation had its own structure, systems, personnel, traditions, and fields of work—it was not feasible or desirable to merge them. Each would continue to grow independently. But at Dehra Dun in India they would create the first Ryder-Cheshire project, a settlement run by a new joint venture. They would call it Raphael, after the angel of healing described in the Scriptures.[3]

The land for the project lay outside the city of Dehra Dun—it included an area sometimes called The Dip as it lay in a fold of hills and could not usually be seen. Here a pitiful collection of people had gathered over the years—people who had come hoping to be cured of leprosy but

---

[3]   The name Raphael means "God heals". The Book of Tobit describes how God sent the Archangel Raphael to help Tobit and his family.

had been disappointed and, unable to return home because of the stigma of the disease, remained and lived in poverty in makeshift housing and with no proper facilities or status. Leonard Cheshire would later write:

> Somehow the combination of such a degree of poverty with the fact of being ostracised had the effect of creating a common solidarity. Certainly I was not prepared for the extraordinary and spontaneous warmth of their welcome.[4]

When he visited to discuss plans he was welcomed with great enthusiasm, and draped with garlands of marigolds while speeches were made—the people were not only showing their gratitude but were anxious to offer their own help and support in every way they could as the project went ahead.

The district had no access to water or electricity—but support was forthcoming, and slowly the venture got under way. Cheshire returned to Dehra Dun in November 1958 to work on it. From there—and from Singapore where he was also planning projects—he and Sue corresponded, and in January 1959 she joined him in India.

They made a tour of various places where he had already established projects or was planning to do so. Cheshire now felt very much at home in India, and was being given support and encouragement wherever he went. They used an old vehicle: an ambulance that Cheshire had acquired in Singapore and which had been given a makeover by a team from the Indian Army. In typical style they gave it a name, "Ezekiel" after the prophet in the Scriptures.

---

[4]   Quoted in Morris, *Cheshire*, p. 369.

Sue Ryder working with a mobile medical team in India

Their tour ended in Dehra Dun, and it was here that they announced their decision, already by now much discussed, to get married. It was February and they set the wedding date for April. They would marry in India, in a small and unfussy ceremony, and they would start their married life in India.

Knowing that there would be considerable media interest, they wrote to friends to announce the news privately first. They emphasised that they saw their marriage as a deepening of their joint commitment to their work and of extending it.

Both brought great seriousness to the marriage. They had both been brought up in traditional families and had warm relationships with their parents and siblings.[5] Both were

---

[5]   Cheshire had a brief marriage with an American actress when he was young: but as she was herself already married and divorced,

strong patriots with a great sense of commitment to Britain and its traditions. Their Christian faith was central to their lives: from the start of their marriage they would pray together daily, using the traditional prayers of the Church.

Sue Ryder and Leonard Cheshire after their wedding in Bombay (Mumbai)

Sue typically did not spend the next weeks making elaborate wedding preparations. Instead, on returning home from India, she went to Poland and to Czechoslovakia to tackle various projects. In April, she flew to India to join Cheshire, and they were married by the Archbishop of Bombay, Cardinal Valerian Gracias, in his private chapel.[6] There was no walk up the aisle with bridesmaids and pages, just a small gathering of friends. But there was

---

the Church did not recognise their marriage—therefore on meeting Sue Ryder he was entirely free to marry.

6   The date was April 5th. The witnesses were Lawrence Donnelly and Leslie Sawhny.

a brief reception afterwards at Bethlehem House, a Cheshire Home where the patients greeted them with joyful enthusiasm. Then they embarked on a honeymoon in Ryder-Cheshire style—a long train journey to Raphael where more garlands and rejoicing greeted them, followed by a couple of days camping out by a river, cooking for themselves over an open fire. They had wanted to be alone, but were thwarted by a local children's outing and later by an Indian family who needed overnight accommodation.

It was an appropriate start to the Cheshires' married life. They had composed a prayer for their wedding, which was later published, dedicating themselves and their marriage to God:

> To thee, O my God Who art infinite Love
> Yet Who hast called us to be perfect
> even as Thou art perfect:
> Who so loved the World
> that Thou didst give us Thine only begotten Son,
> and who has thereby given Thine all,
> Thine everything:
> Who emptied Thyself of Thy Glory,
> and became obedient unto death,
> even the death of the Cross, for us:
> To Thee
> We surrender our all, our everything,
> to be consumed by the unquenchable fire of Thy Love;
> We desire to love Thee even as Thy
> own Mother loved Thee
> To be generous as Thou alone art generous
> To give our all to Thee as Thou givest Thine to us:
> Thou hast called us O Lord and we have found Thee
> In the poor, the unwanted, and the suffering
> And there we will serve Thee,
> Unto death (CML 278–9).

8 ONWARDS

IN SEPTEMBER 1959, the 20th anniversary of the outbreak of World War II, the Cheshires led a pilgrimage
to Dachau, the notorious Nazi concentration camp
on the outskirts of Munich. This was one of the first events
organised by the new Ryder-Cheshire Foundation. Accompanied by a priest who had himself been imprisoned at
Dachau, Sue and the group flew from Blackbushe airport
in Britain to Munich where they met Cheshire. At the
camp they walked in solemn procession to pray where so
many thousands had died. An all-night vigil was held. A
Pathé News film recorded the scenes and this was shown
at cinemas across Britain. The reporter describing the
pilgrimage finished by focusing on a statue of Christ and
commenting: "Men like Cheshire—and in a lesser way
everyday people—teach that salvation lies not in worldly
power, but in the abiding virtues divinely inspired."[1]

Throughout the next years, Sue's work expanded. Much
was happening in Poland and she was a frequent visitor
there. The authorities knew and respected her and she
always found a welcome and a sense of refuge at Konstancin, which was growing and flourishing, with young
women receiving good medical care and also opportunities
to make new lives free from the restrictions to which
disability had bound them.

In Britain the Sue Ryder Foundation was by now part of
the lives of thousands. For many years its Chairman was

---

[1]   British Pathé News was the news service with films shown daily
at cinemas, especially those situated at or near railway stations,
before television had become standard for everyone.

Harry Sporborg CMG CH,[2] whom Sue had initially met
through SOE—of which he was deputy head—during the
War, when she was on a brief visit to Baker Street. When
she later approached him for possible help with her Foundation he not only agreed but remained a loyal and effective
Chairman for the next three decades, overseeing massive
expansion and development. Sue would later recall:

> He was one of those rare people who had absolute
> integrity. A quiet man, he never published anything
> on his work with SOE because he considered that
> the interests of security prevented him from doing
> this…After becoming Chairman of the Foundation
> Harry witnessed its rapid growth in Britain and
> overseas. He was a good listener, a born leader and
> always a wise counsellor and a true friend to me
> and to the members of the Council… (CML 492).

The headquarters of the Foundation remained at Cavendish, where the Cheshires now also had their home. It was
a couple of small rooms at the top of the house, with a
space on the landing for a table where they ate their meals.
The rest of the house was entirely devoted to the residents,
and when their two children, Jeromy and Elizabeth ("Gigi")
were born in 1960 and 1962 respectively, they grew up as
part of this wider community.

Gigi would later recall a happy childhood, with the
house busy with residents, relays of local ladies arriving to
cook, and teams of young people coming to volunteer in
the summer: "It was an amazing place." Family life was
centred on the small flat on the top floor—both children

---

[2]   CMG: Companion of the Order of St Michael and St George.
        The further initials CH stand for Companion of Honour, an
        honour awarded for acts of conspicuous national importance.
        Membership of the Companions of Honour is limited to 65
        people at any one time and is one of the highest honours that can
        be awarded.

were born there—but extended through the house. Although Leonard was frequently travelling, he was close to his children and Gigi recalled:

> He did everything dads do. He took us to school, did the washing up. He was away a lot giving talks and visiting homes but when he was home, he was hands-on, always present and gave you his full attention. He was a wonderful father...[3]

The children made friends among the residents and volunteers, and had full run of the extensive grounds. Other relatives were not far away—Sue's brother Stephen had a farm in Suffolk—and were regular visitors.

With newborn Jeromy in 1960

---

[3] *Daily Mirror,* 7 August 2020.

By the start of the 1960s, there were long waiting lists for the beds at Cavendish—it was answering a crucial need. There were requests for places for patients discharged from hospital who had nowhere to go, handicapped people whose families could not care for them, people with long-term disabilities who needed a place where they could feel at home. It had become well known, and had a good reputation for its family atmosphere and sense of welcome.

The pressure on space—although further extensions were made to the house—made Sue look further afield for new possibilities. In 1961 the Sue Ryder Foundation acquired Hickleton Hall in Yorkshire.[4] It was a magnificent building owned by a famous family earlier in the century—in the 1920s Lord Halifax had been a leading figure seeking Christian unity and a number of important meetings were held there—but by 1960 it was in a poor state of repair. Sue would later recall that she liked it because the kitchen's stone floors brought back childhood memories. The whole place needed a great deal of work—but the place that the Hall held in local loyalties brought huge numbers of volunteers. Teams of people arrived, bringing gifts of food, full of enthusiasm and keen to start work cleaning and painting the rooms. It was not just individuals and families—local voluntary groups and organisations were quickly involved, and everyone had their own ideas on what needed to be done. Sue and her Foundation staff had to insist on basic repairs being done first, and on people entering by the main door (they ended up having to block off the other doors) and giving their names, addresses and work skills so that the project would operate properly. There were over sixty rooms that needed to be re-plas-

---

4   Its story dates back to the 16th century, and the present house was built in 1745.

tered. There was no hot water available and just one small primus stove. There was no furniture except for one table.

Once work could begin it became a massive local enterprise. People donated furniture—including a total of 75 double beds, and thirty harmoniums! Organised into teams and allocated specific rooms on which to work, they plastered and painted and cleaned. Local firms provided paint and other items at well below market prices. Miners working in the local pits came after their shifts to help. Sue never forgot this experience:

> The kindness and willingness of the local people were overwhelming... There was a great sense of unity and friendship... The perpetual coal dust reminded me of my childhood in Yorkshire, and memories of Scarcroft and of other places in the West Riding came flooding back (CML 525).

Hickleton became a flagship for the Foundation, giving high-quality care for resident patients and running a popular day-care centre.[5] Molly Trim who had left her native New Zealand in the late 1950s became House Mother of Hickleton and remained a close friend and supporter of Sue and her work for over fifty years.

As the Homes and linked activities expanded, the Foundation itself also took shape and became effectively a community with its own message echoing Sue's own strongly-held values. A magazine, *Remembrance,* went regularly to subscribers, carrying news of activities and reporting on the enthusiastic fund-raising efforts by hundreds of people. Over the next years such fund-raising expanded to become a major part of national life: Rotary

---

[5]   Hickleton Hall flourished as a Sue Ryder Home until 2012 when changing needs meant that its residential care was no longer suitable and it was sold: it is currently divided into large apartments in private hands.

Clubs and Scouts and Guides, churches and sports associations, schools, clubs and individuals all found the Sue
Ryder Foundation something with which they could
identify. There were sponsored walks—sometimes on a
massive scale with people making their way across Europe
on pilgrimage—concerts, dinners, coffee-mornings, fetes
and bazaars, raffles, and sports events.

The establishment of Sue Ryder shops opened a further
chapter—and not only raised funds for the Foundation
but provided a useful service for millions of people. They
could donate items they no longer needed—everything
from a wedding dress or a collection of books to a side-
board, a boxful of toys, a sewing machine or stacks of
plates or saucepans—knowing that they were helping a
good cause. Everything donated in good condition would
be sold at a modest price and the shops became a familiar
sight in Britain's High Streets. Almost as important, they
provided opportunities for voluntary service and became
important in community life. Beginning in the late 1950s,
the network of shops expanded rapidly—some large towns
had more than a dozen of them. A structure of regional
managers ensured high standards and there were regular
meetings and training for staff.

Sue relished the practical side of all this: helping to
unpack the boxes of goods arriving at Cavendish became a
satisfying task and echoed deeply with her sense of thrift
and frugality. All her life—starting in a 1920s childhood
helping her mother with work among the poorest local
families—she had been encouraged to make good use of
everything that might be useful, and to dislike waste. Being
physically involved with the sorting of the second-hand
goods was energising to her and she also enjoyed the sense
of order and purpose that was essential to the smooth
running of the whole Foundation. She oversaw the system-

atic mailing-out of *Remembrance* magazine and of personalised Christmas cards to supporters (she signed hundreds of these, starting in the early autumn each year), the keeping of careful records, and the despatching of the vast quantities of good-quality second-hand goods to shops. All this formed part of a regular structure that framed her days.

While the theme of the Sue Ryder Foundation was "Remembrance" and the symbol was a sprig of rosemary, Sue was also looking ahead. As the 1960s advanced, and it was known that the lease of the house at Long Melford in Suffolk would run out in due course, Sue needed somewhere new for her holiday scheme for concentration camp victims and for others needing care.

She spent much time visiting possible properties. Many proved far too expensive or in danger of collapse through damp and neglect. Finally, one brochure listed Stagenhoe, on the outskirts of Hitchin in Hertfordshire, which proved suitable. Its history dated back to the Domesday Book and 19th century owners included Sir Arthur Sullivan of "Gilbert and Sullivan" fame. By the 1960s it was empty and in a poor condition, but its fine rooms and beautiful grounds made it ideal for Sue's purposes. Negotiations began and the Foundation bought the building.

In the summer of 1969 a group of concentration camp survivors was due to arrive for a holiday but the house was not ready. In a generous gesture, members of the Rotary Club in Weybridge, Surrey offered to host the visitors in their own homes. This gave a breathing-space to get Stagenhoe into a usable state, and a team of volunteers arrived to work round the clock, cleaning out the drains, creating a functioning water system, repairing the electric wiring, clearing the chimneys, and more. Gifts, including carpets and furniture, began to arrive, and a team of local Venture Scouts tackled the overgrown grounds, using scythes and then mowing the huge lawns. Meanwhile the holidaying group from Poland enjoyed trips and outings, meals and concerts with their Rotary hosts, and on the final two days of the visit, were able to gather at Stagenhoe and become its first guests. By tradition, the final evening of every holiday group was devoted to music, recitations and speeches, sealing friendships which went on to last, often into the next generation.

Over the next years more than 2,500 visitors from Poland stayed at Stagenhoe. The system was by this stage being organised from Poland by volunteers who were themselves concentration camp survivors and included doctors and other medical workers. They drew up lists of people who might need a holiday break and visited them, and in doing so recorded many stories of tragic experiences in forced-labour camps, prisons, and elsewhere. Among much else, Sue's work was resulting in the compilation of information of extraordinary importance for history.

International Family Day at Stagenhoe in 1975

Stagenhoe also became a home for handicapped people, initially for those requiring a short stay, and then later for permanent residents. From across Britain, sufferers from muscular dystrophy, strokes, multiple sclerosis and, in particular Huntington's chorea, applied for care. With its up-to-date community facilities, it also became a centre for meetings and conferences, where all sorts of groups, from the Duke of Edinburgh's Award Scheme to Anglican bishops, could meet and make use of the beautiful rooms and grounds.

9 PART OF BRITISH LIFE

IN 1969 ROBERT Clifton, a Norwich solicitor, began what was to become a decades-long involvement with the Sue Ryder Foundation.

> My father had been involved with a Norfolk Cheshire Home and after he died in 1966 they asked me if I would join the committee: I became chairman, and got to know Leonard Cheshire well. I loved the work and wondered if I could serve the organisation in some full-time way. I mentioned this to Leonard and he said there was no position available—only voluntary appointments of the type I already held—but that he would talk to his wife, who was looking for some help for her own Foundation.
>
> So I met the Cheshires—they brought the children to the Cheshire Home where I was chairman—and we talked. Sue Ryder explained that her work was expanding rapidly, especially overseas, and she needed to ensure that the presence in Britain remained strong. At that time there were three homes in Britain—the idea was to look after these three and to open some new ones. I became her personal assistant and that's how it all began.[1]

The first new project was a Home at Oxenhope near Keighley in Yorkshire for cancer patients, and this was soon followed by a Home at Nettlebed in Oxfordshire.

> Sue called a conference at the start of the 1970s to talk about cancer care, and to identify areas of the

---

[1]   Conversation with author, Dec 2020. Robert Clifton was later ordained to the Anglican ministry and leads retreats and prayer gatherings for the Sue Ryder Prayer Fellowship.

country where accommodation for cancer patients was needed: 'SOS areas' we called them. That was how we acquired Nettlebed. It had been used as a convalescent home for St Mary's Hospital in Paddington. Lord Ennals, who was the Secretary of State for Health, knew us as he had worked as a volunteer at a Sue Ryder project in Germany so he put us in contact with the Nettlebed people. We paid very little for the house and it was in good condition, and had 20 beds. The area was in desperate need of places for cancer care and we were able to provide it.

The house, Jacobean in style, dates from the 19th century and its name is Joyce Grove. It had for some years been owned by the Fleming family, and Ian Fleming, creator of the fictional spy James Bond, spent much of his childhood there. Its last owner, Peter Fleming—uncle of Ian—had given the house to St Mary's hospital. Unlike many of the houses acquired by the Sue Ryder Foundation, it did not require massive renovation work and could be adapted with reasonable ease for cancer care.[2]

Over the next years the number of Sue Ryder Homes in Britain grew steadily. Each had its own story, and each included the deep involvement of local people, who became loyally attached to the Home.

Probably the biggest adventure came with Leckhampton Court, Gloucestershire. This 14th century Cotswold manor house[3] had belonged to the Elwes family and during

---

[2]   The hospice at Nettlebed, opened in 1979, closed in March 2020 after requests for beds declined and surveys showed most people preferred to remain in their own homes to receive treatment. The Sue Ryder organisation now offers care from the Sue Ryder Duchess of Kent Hospice in Reading and outpatients clinics in Newbury and Wokingham.

[3]   The story of the house dates back to the Giffard family who were Lords of the local manor from the 1330s. In more recent times

the First World War had been used as a hospital for wounded soldiers. But it had subsequently fallen into disrepair and by the time Sue Ryder and Robert Clifton went to look at it with the idea of acquiring it as a Home, it was on the "endangered list" of Britain's historic houses and seemed likely to be demolished.

"We had difficulty in finding it" Robert Clifton would later recall.

> It was completely hidden by the huge overgrown trees. We knew where the house was but couldn't see any glimpse of it. We literally had to crawl on all fours through the bushes and the thick under-growth in order to discover it. When we did, we found it was in a very bad state: it even had a tree growing right through it. A great sycamore, going up through the roof.[4]

Sue would later describe her relief at the news of the collapse of the roof of one part of the ancient house, which at least meant the rest could be saved and restored. Surveys were carried out and it was decided to restore the stable block first, so that it could be used as a base from which to work on the rest. The stable had been home for some years to a flock of geese belonging to the Saunders family, the former owners, and over the next weeks acquired the nickname Goose Bay. A new home was found for the birds at the bottom of the drive though they were reluctant to leave and had to be carried there one by one.

A local appeal committee was formed to raise funds, and worked with great energy, eventually raising more than the target of £150,000. A building firm, Thomas Williams (Loughborough) of Moreton-in-Marsh proved exception-

---

it has been used by the Army in World War II and then run as a preparatory school in the 1950s.

[4]   Robert Clifton, Conversation with author, December 2020.

ally helpful, with the company's senior partner Cecil Williams going on to become Chairman of Leckhampton Court's House Committee. Site meetings took place in one usable room, by a log fire, with Joan Williams providing lunch, and everyone on planks around a makeshift table. (CML 578–579). They nicknamed the project "Pilgrim's Progress". By 1981 it was ready to receive the first patients, and in 1988 Goose Bay was opened as a Day Care Centre.

While all this was happening, Leonard's Cheshire Homes across Britain were also flourishing and expanding in number, and the Ryder-Cheshire Foundation was active in India and elsewhere—while in Poland Sue's work had grown and grown and now involved large numbers of people, all of whom knew of her and of her association with the cause of Poland in World War II and beyond.

In Britain the Ryder-Cheshire pair were themselves now in effect a national institution. Their work, along with their eccentricities of a simple and unpretentious lifestyle coupled with old-fashioned commitment to patriotism, the Monarchy, and the Church, made them popular and at times even venerated. Leonard Cheshire was much in demand as a speaker and lecturer, and his thoughts on God, suffering, death, hope, and the meaning of life, were read and discussed. It came as no surprise when in 1978 Sue was honoured by being created a life peeress in her own right. After considerable uncertainty and after discussion with her husband and Harry Sporborg, chairman of the Foundation, she decided to accept, seeing the possibilities of membership of the House of Lords as a way of focusing attention on the needs of the people she had always sought to help.

Sue made history by deciding to take, as her title, not the name of a British city or county as was customary, but the name of Poland's capital, Warsaw, in tribute to Poland's wartime heroism. This required special permission from the Queen and a discussion with the Polish ambassador. When she entered the House of Lords, robed and announced in formal style, the long years of work for Poles found recognition and a voice.

Sue's story seemed to have reached a climax. The Ryder-Cheshire partnership had created something unique and it was all now flourishing. But the story was not yet over, and as they approached later life, both were still active and ready for new work and new ventures.

The Cavendish house was expanded and altered over the years. A major ground floor addition included a larger kitchen, and communal dining room, together with more bedrooms. The number of staff also expanded to cope with the considerable administration involved with what was now a major international organisation. All the office staff shared the house with the residents and volunteers. In later years Sue looked back with nostalgia to the very earliest days when all the staff ate together in a cramped kitchen in relays.

For many years, Sue's secretary was June Backler, who joined the Foundation in 1972 and became a close friend as well as a dedicated colleague. There were staff working full-time on accounts, legal issues, the covenant gift scheme and more.

Ruth Young began involvement with the Sue Ryder Foundation as a young volunteer, and then took up a full-time post at Cavendish in the late 1980s, working in the administration office.

> The arrival of the post each day was the big thing. It arrived early—about 6am—and the Polish volunteers would be there to help deal with it. Lady Ryder—we always called her that, never Sue—was always already up and busy. She got up at 4am.

The volunteers included older retired people—I remember one lady whose husband had been in Auschwitz. There were also young people who came from Poland in groups—some of them had grandparents who had been in the war and in concentration camps.[5]

The Sue Ryder Foundation by now had a catalogue that was posted out and people could order Christmas cards. Dealing with the post each day included packing and posting the cards ordered from the catalogue, and also banking the large number of donations. There were also regular arrivals of second-hand clothes and other items destined for the Sue Ryder shops. Sue relished dealing with these, and took an active part in all the work, as did Leonard when at home. Clothes were checked, and if necessary washed, ironed and repaired at Cavendish—sometimes in the Cheshires' own washing machine in their small flat— before being bagged and labelled for the various shops. Ruth Young remembered Sue as a lively presence:

She was a tiny figure, and in my memory always looked rather tired. She was active all the time, and we were all kept busy too. Every day she would go to Mass at 10 am—either in the chapel at the house, or to the Priory at Clare.

During the 1980s the layout of the rooms at Cavendish changed further as extensions and alterations to the house were carried out. There was a museum which told the story of Sue's life and the establishment of the Foundation, including a replica of a room from her childhood home, a display about World War II and the FANY, and pictures of Poland's devastation and of Warsaw being rebuilt. There were also handcrafts made by residents at various

---

[5]   Ruth Young, conversation with author, December 2020

Homes, gifts presented to Sue Ryder over the years, and pictures of major events including Royal visits.

Sue was still driving regularly to Poland—but the whole operation had grown and flourished. The rapidly changing situation there began with the election of Pope John Paul— the first Polish Pope in history—in 1978 followed by the creation of the Solidarity Movement in 1980. Then followed the moves towards freedom over the next years, and the Communist response with the imposition of martial law. This law meant that there were shortages of food and other essentials, and several different groups and organisations in Western Europe and America organised relief supplies.

An audience with Pope—now Saint—John Paul II

Throughout the 1980s there were constant arrivals and departures of what became a fleet of lorries taking goods to Poland. Volunteer drivers took the packed vehicles across the Channel and along the motorways of Europe, taking goods that ranged from clothes and household necessities to medicines, antiseptics, and equipment for handicapped people. All of this was accompanied by much publicity: Poland was no longer the "forgotten ally" of the 1950s but a country at the forefront of people's minds with its plight, and its future, much discussed and with people in Britain eager to help.

Packed and ready: the van filled with goods for Poland, outside the Headquarters at Cavendish

The Sue Ryder homes and shops became collecting centres for food and supplies. Lorry loads would leave Cavendish each week for Poland. Meanwhile Sue Ryder herself was buying food in bulk on the international wholesale food markets in Europe and sending it to Poland.

Sue with her van "Joshua" on one of the long drives across Europe: she often had to struggle against bitter weather

In 1989 came the great changes in Eastern Europe—the "Velvet Revolution" in Czechoslovakia, full freedom in Poland, independence for the Baltic States, and in due course the destruction of the Berlin Wall, and the collapse of the Soviet Union. Communism, which had brought so much misery to Russia and to Eastern Europe, had collapsed. The 1990s would provide new hopes, and new challenges.

10 CHALLENGES, CHANGES, AND A CLOSING CHAPTER

POLISH-BORN HALINA KENT had arrived in Britain as a post-war child refugee with her family. In 1990, her husband spotted a notice in the Polish-language weekly newspaper they regularly read, inviting applications for a position with the Sue Ryder Foundation's work.

> I remember going to Cavendish and waiting for a long time because Sue Ryder was busy. When we met, she didn't mince her words. "I want you to go to Poland and find volunteers." The idea was to set up Sue Ryder shops in Poland, and register a Polish Foundation.
>
> I hadn't been to Poland since 1946. My husband came with me: we had no budget, no hotel or travel expenses, nothing except a letter of reference from Sue. But it was astonishing: I had no idea how well known she was in Poland. I was given access to Lech Walesa's office—he had just been elected as Prime Minister—and when I told them I needed help they contacted twenty local authorities across the country. I also met Cardinal Glemp, the Archbishop of Warsaw, who thought very highly of Sue Ryder. From those initial contacts came the first three charity shops—in the early days we had to bring the clothes and other items out from England, but in due course they ran things on their own.
>
> Establishing a voluntary organisation in newly post-Communist Poland proved a challenge. I had to discover what the laws were, and what I needed to do. The situation was new to the Poles at that

time—under Communism the whole idea of voluntary service had been regarded as humiliating. It was something that, for example, criminals might be made to do. The idea of an independent voluntary group was something that had to be explained. But I managed to register the Foundation—and everywhere I found that people knew about Sue Ryder and would help.

Communism was a terrible system. People learned not to trust one another. And no one dared to take initiatives, or to take responsibility for things. Sometimes even within a family people didn't dare to talk freely.[1]

As the Foundation slowly became established in Poland, people in Britain were generous with support. In Burgess Hill, Sussex, where Halina and her husband lived, local people and shops donated gifts—including a wedding shop which donated a wedding gown. There was television coverage, and further support poured in.

The first Polish charity shop was established in Poznan, and Sue was there to open it, driving as usual with a vanload of goods for this and other projects.

Working with her, you realised that her life was a response to a call. She just opened her heart to anyone in need. To see her with people who were sick was a real lesson in humanity.

She had no time for any frivolities or luxuries. She would never stay in an hotel—we knew this and she was offered a room next to a church. Everyone was keen to help—her name was immediately recognised everywhere in Poland.

---

[1]   Conversation with author December 2020.

Sue Ryder with girls from Konstancin on their visit to England

Back in Britain, the Cheshires continued to live in their small flat at Cavendish, with Sue working daily at her office on the ground floor. There were travels to the different countries where their joint and separate projects were established: Australia, New Zealand, Japan, India—the work was now worldwide. At home, the work of the Sue Ryder Foundation continued, with Homes to visit, shop managers and group leaders to meet, catalogues and other publications to discuss, and vast quantities of donated goods to be sent to different destinations. *Remembrance* continued to be published, and new initiatives for fund-raising were starting all the time, from coach trips to sponsored events.

Journalist Alenka Lawrence stayed with the Cheshires at Cavendish in 1990 to interview Leonard for a book about his ideals and beliefs. She was struck by the extraor-

dinary mixture of deep Christian warmth, combined with
a certain old-fashioned formal style.

> The welcome in the old rambling house was kind
> and sincere. I felt, talking to Leonard Cheshire, that
> I was in the presence of a man who had something
> deeply important to convey about the great issues
> facing us all.
>
> Around the rest of the house you were conscious
> of Sue Ryder's presence. There were notes asking
> for certain things to be done—something mended
> in one of the rooms, or whatever—signed,
> somehow rather emphatically, "Ryder of Warsaw!"
> Our paths hardly crossed but one day, when I was
> sitting interviewing Leonard, his face suddenly lit
> up. He looked over my shoulder and called
> out, "Darling!" I turned around and there was this
> small figure dressed simply, like a housekeeper. She
> asked him a quick question and then left again.[2]

Lawrence's interviews with Cheshire were published as a
book *Where is God in all this?*[3] exploring thoughts on God,
death, hope, and the meaning of suffering. It would prove
to be among Cheshire's last public messages. Always
subject to ill health, he was now increasingly frail. Unde-
terred by this, he made a trip to India, to visit his beloved
Raphael at Dehra Dun. By this time he was in a wheelchair,
and told residents "Now I am like one of you. I know the
hardships and mental trauma that all of you are going
through". As he left India he kissed the ground: it was a
place that meant so much to him and to Sue.[4]

---

[2]   Conversation with the author, 2021.
[3]   London, St Pauls Publishing, 1991.
[4]   J. Beslièvre et al, *"Still the Candle Burns"* (St Helier: Jersey
       Cheshire Home Foundation, 1997).

Leonard Cheshire died in July 1992 at the age of 74: he had been made a life peer the year before[5], the last in the many honours bestowed on him which included the Order of Merit. He had suffered from several severe illnesses in his life and his last months were marked by motor neurone disease. Working right to the end, he retained his commitment to honouring all who had served Britain in war, helping to establish the National Memorial Arboretum in Staffordshire where the amphitheatre is named after him.

The many tributes to Cheshire included one from the Queen, who devoted part of her annual Christmas broadcast in 1992 to him. Among many others, former Prime Minister Lord Callaghan of Cardiff referred specifically to Sue in his tribute in the House of Lords:

> Leonard met and married Sue Ryder, a kindred spirit, whose dedicated work for the survivors of Nazi concentration camps, together with her other international relief work, complemented his own efforts... Their aspirations grew and, against all the odds, they established an astonishing number of Homes throughout the world...All her friends and many who knew him only through his work send their affection and sorrow at the ending of her partnership with a very great man, and salute her courage in continuing with the tasks to which they were jointly pledged.[6]

Sue continued to travel, visiting Ryder-Cheshire projects. Her responsibilities in the House of Lords also took up much of her time: she was active in debates on child care, drug abuse, medical issues and social welfare. She spoke up in defence of traditional Christian teachings on mar-

---

[5]   He took the title Baron Cheshire of Woodhall in the county of Lincolnshire.

[6]   Reprinted in Beslièvre, *Still the Candle Burns*.

riage, family, and the protection of life—both she and Leonard had been strongly opposed to both abortion and euthanasia.

In her autobiography, first published in 1986 and then revised and updated in 1997, she wrote of her sadness at the abandonment of prayers in hospitals and elsewhere:

> I find it very hard indeed to accept the growing secular emphasis in Britain, the lack of any religious instruction or reference to God at school or in life. This breeds indifference to all things spiritual and can lead to the wasteland of materialism where violence is inevitable and self-gratification is the only goal (CML 609).

The establishment of the Sue Ryder Prayer Fellowship as a separate charity meant a great deal to her: men and women from different Christian denominations meeting at Walsingham and, later, at St Katharine's, Parmoor, near Henley-on-Thames for retreats and days of prayer[7]. She wrote:

> Britain ... has been a Christian country for many centuries and drawn moral strength from its convictions. The beauty of our literature, music and art is enriched with its traditions and if we were to lose all this, we would indeed be the poorer, and I feel completely wrong too (CML 610).

---

[7]   St Katharine's is a Christian retreat centre, open to individuals and groups of all faiths and none, run by the Sue Ryder Prayer Fellowship. It is a large country house, owned at one time by Charles Alfred Cripps QC whose guests over the years included Lord Baden-Powell, Albert Einstein, Emperor Haile Selassie, and Indira Ghandi. On his death it was let for some years to the exiled King Zog of Albania, and it was then acquired by an Anglican religious community of sisters who had been bombed out of their London convent. The sisters gifted the house to the Prayer Fellowship and it was legally transferred in 1998.

In 1998 the John Moores University in Liverpool made Sue an Honorary Fellow in a ceremony chaired by Lord Alton,[8] Professor of Citizenship at the University. In his speech he noted Sue's various honours including Companion of the Order of St Michael and St George, OBE, and the papal Pro Ecclesia et Pontifice and added that she liked to describe herself as "just a truck driver". Lord Alton worked with Sue in the House on Lords where they shared many interests in humanitarian causes, and his wife coincidentally had spent some years working with Leonard Cheshire.

As the 1990s ended, Sue had the sorrow of deep disagreements with the Trustees of her Foundation. While recognising the need for changes, she saw herself as the guardian of the organisation's founding principles, including personal care, frugality, deep personal commitment, and an emphasis on community and neighbourly help. Demands for more aggressive approaches to the running of the charity shops, or for ruthless abandonment of projects that seemed old-fashioned were to her a rejection of the ideals and beliefs at the core of the work. Publicity surrounding the split with the organisation was saddening for all. Eventually Sue, by this stage frail and unwell, established a new organisation with the thought that it could continue to fund some projects. This took shape in 2000 as the Bouverie Foundation and is now (in 2022) the Lady Ryder of Warsaw Memorial Trust. But this was not the end of the story: her original organisation continued (and continues) to bear her name, and hundreds of people benefit from the many Homes and projects that she initiated and ran: the work lives on.

---

[8]   David Alton, b. 1951, was a Liverpool Member of Parliament for 18 years, before standing down in 1997 and being appointed a Life Peer. At John Moores University he established the Foundation for Citizenship and the Rose Lectures. He is the author of several books.

Sue Ryder died in 2000, aged 76. There were tributes to her around the world, recalling her extraordinary life and her dedication to the cause of the relief of suffering.

Among many obituaries, after describing her wartime service, her work with concentration camp victims, the foundation of her Homes, and more, one summed her up:

> She was without fear, moral or physical, ate little, slept little, was completely indifferent to her own comfort, and often looked exhausted yet she seemed borne on by some inner fire of strength. She dictated and signed innumerable letters, spoke at countless meetings, appeared on radio and television, was interviewed by the press ... and always continued her personal role of "mamusia" "mother"—as the Poles called her—for each of her charges.[9]

When giving any talk about her work, Sue always liked to end with some words of Reverend Mother Stuart:

> We have to prepare for the future, and yet we do not know what it will bring.
>
> We have to find a standing ground so firm that nothing unexpected can disturb us, and so broad that it will carry any undertaking that we may have to base upon it, and so satisfying that it will take the place of all other satisfactions.
>
> There is only one thing that answers to this and that is the Will of God.[10]

But perhaps the last word should be given to Sue herself. In old age she wrote:

> I am conscious of my own immortality, and that whatever we do, does count, not only here and now

---

[9]   *The Guardian*, 3 November 2000.
[10] Quoted in CML 612.

but in that great future for which we have all been created. It may sometimes be that we are given that certain opportunity only once and if we fail to respond it will not be given to us again. But if we seize the opportunity, even if we should not succeed in achieving our goal, the effort involved can be offered up to God who is our judge and who is able to turn every defeat into victory (CML 608–609).

Part Two
The Work Continues

THE WORK CONTINUES

Message from the Trustees of the Lady Ryder of Warsaw Memorial Trust

SUE RYDER'S EARLY life and wartime experiences set her on a remarkable journey to work tirelessly for the rest of her life to relieve suffering. This took her to many countries over the years.

The work started almost immediately at the end of the Second World War in 1946, and Sue Ryder established it as a Living Memorial to all the millions who gave their lives during two World Wars in defence of human values, and to the countless others who are suffering and dying today as a result of persecution, hunger and disease. Some of the projects were short-term but in most countries where she worked there are projects which continue to flourish today. They are the Living Memorial that Sue Ryder always intended.

We are unsure if this list is exhaustive: we have tried to cover every country and every project, but cannot be certain as her scope was wide. In addition, since 1945 some countries have changed shape or have had various changes of government. For example, there were many homes and missions in the former Yugoslavia; the work continues in the various independent countries which now exist but for the purposes of this book we have listed them together.

Sue Ryder gave everyone she met a very warm and personal feeling of particular interest and individual care. Her enthusiasm, charity and sense of neighbourly care extended to projects across the world. Clearly because of her wartime experiences and its pressing post-war needs,

Poland was always close to her heart, and consequently we have placed it first in the list which follows, but after that, countries are listed in alphabetical order. Details of the work of the Lady Ryder of Warsaw Memorial Trust are given under the United Kingdom section.

Most of these projects have been funded, according to Sue Ryder's own ideas, from gifts and local philanthropy. Her initiative of charity shops started in the UK and still to this day funds much of the work of Sue Ryder (the name for the current group of neurological care centres and hospices, previously known as Sue Ryder Care and an independent organisation in its own right) in Britain.

It is impossible to say how many people's lives have been helped or influenced by Sue Ryder and her continuing work: it must be hundreds of thousands of individuals.

The trustees of the Lady Ryder of Warsaw Memorial Trust, are proud to set out the details in this biography marking the centenary of Sue Ryder's birth. The details and figures were compiled as at January 2022. We continue her work where we can by providing funds to worthwhile causes, notably the establishments she founded overseas.

POLAND

S UE RYDER STARTED work in Poland soon after the end
of the Second World War. She worked with the local
and national health authorities in the provision of
Homes—for all ages including those with physical disabilities, psychological problems and for those undergoing
treatment for cancer. Often the local authorities already
had a hospital or centre in existence and the Foundation
built a Home on the site. These took the form of pavilions—
prefabricated buildings sent out from the UK, together with
equipment. The local authorities were responsible for the
foundation of the buildings and the plumbing and electrics.
Volunteer tradesmen from the UK were sent to Poland to
assemble the pavilions and these became the Sue Ryder
Homes in Poland. At the time of Sue Ryder's death, there
were 28 homes across the country. In some cases, there
were more than one Home in each place.

The first Home was at Konstancin in a district of
Warsaw and was opened in 1957. This was for girls and
young women suffering from rheumatoid arthritis. Here
they were able to receive treatment at the nearby Institute
of Rheumatology and to continue with education and to
work in the workshop in the Home, making dolls in folk
costumes to sell. Many of them went on to lead independent lives.

Bydgoszcz

In 1963 the first independent Oncology department in
Bydgoszcz was established. The first Sue Ryder pavilion
was built in the 1960s in the grounds of the Dr A Jurasz

Hospital and a second pavilion was built at Fordon. In 1996, a new Sue Ryder Home was opened in the grounds of the regional Oncology centre in Bydgoszcz. Palliative and hospice care for adults and children. 37 in-patient beds, as well as hospice at home care.

Gdynia Redlowo

Sue Ryder Home built in the 1990s in a wing of the Oncology Hospital.

Góra Kalwaria

South of Warsaw, a Social Welfare Home established in 1840. Three Sue Ryder pavilions built in the 1960s with 70 beds for those with chronic physical or mental illness.

Gorno

Sanatorium in Gorno established in 1949 and is now the John Paul ll Healthcare Institute Complex. As part of the complex, the Sue Ryder hospice offering palliative care opened in 2001 with two in-patient beds.

Helenow

In part of Warsaw, a complex of schools and rehabilitation centres established in 1922 by the Society of Friends. The first Sue Ryder pavilion was built in 1963 and a replacement was built in 2012 for the kindergarten. 180–200 children are looked after in total, with accommodation for seven children in the Sue Ryder pavilion.

Henryków

Now part of Stołeczny Centrum Opiekuńczo—Leczniczy Sp.zo.o. at Mehoffera Street, Warsaw offering treatment, care and rehabilitation for chronically ill adults who do not require hospitalisation. Established in the 1930s. The three Sue Ryder pavilions were built in the 1960s to accommodate 150 people.

Kałków-Godów

Sue Ryder pavilion built in 2000 to provide nursing care to 80 people who are elderly and for those with chronic conditions.

Konstancin

The Institute of Rheumatology in Warsaw established in 1951. The first of the Sue Ryder pavilions was built in 1957 and the second one in 1966. In the 1990s, two additional pavilions were built.

Popkowicz

Social Welfare Home established in 1950. For the elderly and chronically ill. Sue Ryder pavilion opened in 1971 to accommodate 53 people.

Psarskie

Social Welfare Home established in 1969. Sue Ryder pavilion built in 1973. For chronically ill adults.

Psary

Social Welfare Home established in 1954. Sue Ryder pavilion built in the 1970s to accommodate 55 people. For those with chronic mental illness.

Radzymin

Social welfare home established in 1954 with the two Sue Ryder pavilions built in 1964 and 1969, providing a total of 60 beds. For chronically physically ill people and those with Alzheimers disease.

Zakrzewo

for those with chronic mental illness

Zielona Góra

Sue Ryder hospice for those with terminal illness, especially cancer.

At some time during Sue Ryder's lifetime we believe there were Homes in Radom and Wschowa.

Since Sue Ryder's death, a Home has been built at **Pierzchnica** to care for elderly people in a rural area of the country.

The home for the elderly at Pierzchnica in Poland, named in memory of Sue Ryder

A school at **Niepolomice** has been named in her honour—the first in the world to bear her name. It opened in 2001 and took on Sue Ryder's name in 2003. It caters for 500 pupils aged 7–14.

ALBANIA

Established

1993

History

RYDER ALBANIA ASSOCIATION started in Tirana, providing domiciliary care for terminal cancer patients and the elderly with chronic conditions. In 1996, the work was extended to the city of Durres.

Funding

Sue Ryder UK, Sue Ryder Ireland, the EU and other donors.

Current programme

As a pioneer of palliative care, the Ryder Albania Association has lobbied the central government and local authorities to improve the quality of service provided to terminally ill patients. This has resulted in the establishment of a national strategy for palliative care, funded medication, and fully-approved standards of service.

Services provided

Ryder Albania Association provides a service to about 90 terminally-ill patients per day: some 50 patients in Tirana and 40 in Durrës, a total of some 450 per year.

Staff

The Tirana team established in 1993 (consisting of three doctors, four nurses and two social workers) and the Durrës team established in 1996 (consisting of two doctors, three nurses and one social worker).

Number of people helped

8,400 (November 1993 to September 2018)—4,400 in Tirana and 4,000 in Durres.

AUSTRALIA

Ryder-Cheshire Australia

IN THE EARLY 1960s following a visit by Sue Ryder and Leonard Cheshire in 1959 soon after their marriage in India. They visited Australia to find donors and support for their project "Raphael" in Dehradun, India. Australians responded and groups were set up around the country to raise money. Ryder-Cheshire Australia (RCA) exists for the primary purpose of funding Raphael and in more recent years, Klibur Domin (in Timor-Leste). The relationship with Klibur Domin was initiated by RCA (Australian Association of Ryder-Cheshire Foundations as it was then) in 2000.

The many committees became affiliated with State Foundations and eventually RCA evolved. This is now the co-ordinating body for the remaining three State Foundations, New South Wales, South Australia and Victoria, and two Support Groups, Ballarat and Bendigo. RCA and its Overseas Aid Fund is managed by a Board of Directors.

In addition, there are two Australian Homes, at Ivanhoe Victoria, and Mount Gambier South Australia. They are quite autonomous and self-funding and each has a representative on the Board of RCA.

As the funding landscape changes so RCA continues to evolve.

Ryder-Cheshire Mount Gambier

Established

2000

History

The local Foundation recognised that in the city of Mount Gambier, population about 27,000, there was an unmet need for supported, independent living accommodation for disabled people. The Ryder-Cheshire Mount Gambier Home Board (run by volunteers) was established and the success of the first home led to the building of a second. In 2000 the Board decided that the homes should provide long term accommodation for people with a range of physical and intellectual disabilities. At the time this was considered unusual but by the time planning started for the second home it was the model preferred by the Federal Government. There are now plans to acquire some land at no cost and once this is achieved, plans to build a new facility.

Services provided

The first home, "Ryder", was opened in 2006. The second home, "Cheshire", in 2018. Each Home provides supported, independent living for five disabled people, women in "Ryder" and men in "Cheshire". The Home Foundation owns the homes and leases them out to ParaQuad SA who provide a 24/7 service to the residents. Each home has five bedrooms, each with an ensuite bathroom. There is a large lounge, a smaller quiet lounge, a dining room, and a large al fresco area, plus spacious gardens including vegetable plots.

Funding and staffing

The ParaQuad SA employs a number of staff, about 10 full time equivalents, to provide the 24/7 services to each home.

Number of people helped

There are ten permanent residents in the two Homes. None have left since they arrived and all are happy with their accommodation.

Ryder-Cheshire Victorian Homes Foundation Inc.

Trading and known as Ryder-Cheshire Ivanhoe

Established

1981

History

On a visit in the 1970s, Sue Ryder and Leonard Cheshire identified a need for a facility to support rural patients—those living sometimes hundreds of miles away from a city hospital—during times of crisis, somewhere for people to stay while attending specialist appointments or undergoing treatment at Melbourne's hospitals.

The Ivanhoe Homes were started by a dedicated group of local volunteers one of whom is the current President of the Committee, Mr Peter Overton. In 1981 they leased the first accommodation block at 12 Donaldson Street, Ivanhoe from the Returned Services League (RSL) of Australia which had built the facility for War Widows. Over the following years, the two adjoining blocks were purchased to provide additional rooms.

Services provided

The Ivanhoe Homes provide low, or no cost, short-term, accommodation for patients and their carers. The Ivanhoe Homes are often described by residents as a "home away from home" where they feel supported and part of a community.

How funded

Everyday running costs are covered by the income generated from residents who stay at the Ivanhoe Homes, some of whom can access government support, otherwise the overnight cost is low. In addition, grants and donations are welcomed.

Extent of land and homes

Built on just over half an acre of land (4725m²) there are three apartment blocks in a quiet street just a few minutes' walk to the shops and public transport and 9km north of Melbourne city centre.

Bedrooms/Services

There are 45 self-contained studio apartments, each with two or three single beds with ensuite bathroom and kitchen. Two of the apartment buildings have lift access, the third has five ground floor wheelchair-accessible rooms.

Other services

All extra services are free and provided by local volunteers or donations and include such things as the use of motorised scooters and bikes to get to and from the shops or appointments. Volunteers are available for a chat or a game of cards and a cup of tea or to help residents with their shopping. In each building there is a communal room and regular weekly morning and afternoon teas are held. At times, the Ivanhoe Homes are privileged to be able to assist the Ryder-Cheshire Foundation Australia in using their facilities to help raise funds to support the homes in Raphael in India and Klibur Domin in Timor-Leste.

Staffing

The original resident carers were lay volunteers. In January 1990 religious sisters took on the position and continued to serve for nearly 30 years. There are now two salaried part-time managers and there is always one Resident Carer in each of the three buildings with someone available 24 hours a day to offer support and assistance. Two of the resident carers for the last 6 years have been international students who donate time in exchange for accommodation. All the Committee members are volunteers and the Homes are staffed and supported by volunteers who donate their time and services for maintenance, domestic and social tasks to keep the Ivanhoe Homes running.

Number of people helped

Over 35,000 people have stayed since the opening of the Ivanhoe Homes. Over the past four years, an average of over 2,000 people a year have stayed.

BELGIUM

I N THE EARLY years, support groups offered hospitality to those travelling on the holiday scheme. In both Brugge and Zebrugge, about six times a year, they met groups of about 40 people who were on their way by train from Poland to England. They carried out fundraising to cover the costs of the hospitality and in the 1970s, Homes were also opened. These were halfway houses for those with psychological disabilities, and were supported by teams of psychiatrists, social workers and lay people.

The Belgian Foundation now has apartments for the short-term care of two families, four specially equipped houses for older couples with disabilities and 10 apartments for people with a mental vulnerability.

It is run entirely by volunteers with funds raised in Sue Ryder Shops.

BELIZE

A TWO-YEAR PROGRAMME IN the early 1980s provided a mobile medical clinic together with a midwife and a nurse.

The funding for this project came largely from the Overseas Service Committee of the Association of Inner Wheel Clubs in Great Britain and Ireland. The mobile clinic was donated by an organisation called Survive.

The Land Rover clinic was christened *Rosemary*, and the nurse and midwife, a local driver and helper based themselves in the village of Benque Viejo. They went out in the bush and carried out vaccinations against whooping cough, diphtheria, and tetanus. They gave training to local people to promote better health, better ante-natal and post-natal care and safer deliveries of babies. They encouraged people to help themselves through information on hygiene and preventative medicine.

At the end of the two years, the programme was handed over to Voluntary Service Overseas who sent out nurses.

The number of people helped cannot be fully listed: many rural communities have been given life-changing assistance, with immunisations and training on the cause, prevention, and treatment of preventable diseases.

CZECHOSLOVAKIA—CZECH REPUBLIC

S UE RYDER STARTED to visit Czechoslovakia after the Second World War to meet ailing and handicapped people. She helped them mainly on an individual basis providing them with wheelchairs and medicines that were not then available in Czechoslovakia. Before 1968 she started to co-operate with the Ministry of Health and Welfare, planning a board of directors and five Sue Ryder homes for those in most need of care. All this had to be abandoned following the Soviet occupation of Czechoslovakia in August 1968.

Soon after the Velvet Revolution and collapse of Communism in 1989, Sue Ryder restarted her effort to establish the Home in Prague. The Czech branch of the Sue Ryder Foundation was registered in the beginning of 1994 and in May of the same year won the tender to establish a Home at the beautiful historic complex of buildings at Michelský dvůr at Michle, in the Prague 4 district, one of the poorest areas of Prague. After extensive rebuilding and renovations the Sue Ryder Home opened to the first elderly residents in 1998.

Services provided

Registered social services

Personal assistance—a home-care service.
Residential care for elderly people in the historic Michelský dvůr Home.

The Home at Michelský dvůr at Michle, in Prague's District 4.

Associated services

Advice, information and practical help including provision of medical equipment, household aids etc.

Social enterprise

7 charity shops in Prague
A restaurant in the Michelský dvůr complex

How funded

The projects are funded by multiple financial sources including public funds, client payments, donations from individuals and organisations, contributions from foundations and endowment funds, fund-raising activities and commercial activities.

The public funds account for a significant part of the Sue Ryder budget, used for the operation and improvement of care quality.

The Sue Ryder charity shops

Network of seven shops across Prague. Other commercial activities of Sue Ryder comprise the operation of the Michelský dvůr restaurant and renting of premises. The revenues used for social services are based on the client payments for accommodation and meals. The amount is limited under the law and thus forms only about 14% of the care costs. For the Sue Ryder operation the donations are indispensable. Support comes from organisations, foundations and endowment funds.

Extent of land and home

Sue Ryder (Prague) is based at the historic complex of Michelský dvůr. It has been reconstructed and is currently used as accommodation for elderly people. In addition, parts are open to the public, including a hall also used as a gallery, a theatre hall (aka the Big Hall), a chapel, the restaurant and one of the Sue Ryder charity shops.

Beds/rooms

The home provides 52 beds for elderly people.

Community work

Sue Ryder (Prague) has been based in the Prague 4 district for over twenty years. The complex is visited by a broad public and there are a number of events all year including jumble sales, craft fairs and special events in the restaurant.

Number of people helped

During the 23 years of the Sue Ryder existence in the Czech Republic more than 34,000 people have been helped.

DENMARK

S UE RYDER HAD contact with supporters in Denmark in the 1950s and 1960s. The Holiday Scheme, for survivors of the concentration camps started in Denmark before transferring to the UK. Supporters, especially members of the Inner Wheel Club continued to raise funds during the early 1970s.

ETHIOPIA

I N 1985 AT the time of the famine crisis in Ethiopia, Sue Ryder worked there with Sisters in Mekele, helping to distribute food, water and medical supplies, as well as helping out in the clinics.

Sue Ryder with children in Ethiopia in 1985

FRANCE

Established in the late 1990s in partnership with Bellevue, Polish Catholic Mission House, Lourdes. In the last years of Sue Ryder's life and following a visit to Lourdes with the Ryder-Cheshire Raphael Pilgrimage, she saw there was a need for accommodation for people with disabilities to stay with their families/carers. In 2005, the Lady Ryder of Warsaw Memorial Trust began working with the Polish Catholic Mission in France and five rooms were built forming a separate wing at Bellevue, specially adapted to accommodate those with disabilities and their families and these were officially opened in May 2009, "The Lady Ryder of Warsaw rooms".

Bellevue is set in its own grounds outside the main pilgrim area of the town, overlooking the Grotto and with views of the Pyrenees. The Lady Ryder of Warsaw Memorial Trust provided funds for a wheelchair-friendly minibus which enables people staying at Bellevue to travel to the centre of Lourdes.

Bellevue is run by an order of nuns. The number of overnight stays to date is 11,000. Most people stay for between 3 and 6 days.

Bellevue, the pilgrim house at Lourdes

GERMANY

S ue Ryder's main work in post-war Germany was prison-visiting. This was extraordinarily difficult work, involving hours of patient negotiations in harsh conditions. Sue's concern was for Polish young men, concentration camp victims who on being liberated had nowhere to live and often resorted to stealing food or other necessities in order to survive as they tried to get home to Poland—and were then cruelly imprisoned in post-war Germany. She offered assistance in court cases, obtaining legal help and giving advice and support to young men who, traumatised and lacking any family or other contacts, found in her a genuine friend. An empty hut on the outskirts of Frankfurt-am-Mein was converted into a Home for these boys, together with a small office from where Sue Ryder could work. This was tragically destroyed in a fire accident, but a disused prison at Bad Nauheim was obtained and converted into a Home.

Sue Ryder's post-war work in Germany would expand to her network of care for large numbers of former victims of concentration camps who would receive support and practical help.

In 1957, St Christopher's Home near Hanover was established. As well as a settlement of eight cottages where permanent residents discharged from hospitals could lead independent lives, often with their families, the Home also acted as a rehabilitation centre for released prisoners. Sue continued to maintain contact with many of her "boys" for the rest of their lives, and through her help many went on to have successful and fulfilling jobs and happy families of their own.

A few of the Boys remained in prison for the remainder of their lives and Sue Ryder continued to visit them every December until the late 1990s, very near to the end of her life, driving alone across Europe. She never forgot them.

GREECE

 T SOME STAGE before 1967 (when there was a coup), the Foundation operated in Greece.

INDIA

Ryder-Cheshire international centre at Dehra-Dun

Established

April 1959

History

RAPHAEL WAS FOUNDED in 1959 in Dehradun (Uttarakhand) jointly by Sue Ryder and Leonard Cheshire. It began by caring for leprosy-cured patients rescued off the streets. Over the years, the civil administration has entrusted Raphael with the care of other persons with disabilities who have nowhere to go. It caters to the needs of the poorer people in the State of Uttarakhand and the neighbouring districts of North Western Uttar Pradesh.

Funding

All services and facilities are provided for free, and Raphael is entirely dependent on its benefactors for funding. Among other donors, Ryder-Cheshire Foundations in Australia and New Zealand raise funds.

Current programmes

Today Raphael's mission is to assist in the rehabilitation of children with intellectual and associated disabilities; control of Tuberculosis (TB); and the life-long care of disabled people who are rejected by society.

Beds/rooms

TB Hospital—20; Residential centre for persons with disabilities—120; 54 quarters for leprosy patients; 35 quarters for employees

Staff

At outset—50; now—105

Number of people helped

60,000

Bangalore

In the late 1960s, Sue Ryder Medical Aid Foundation was established to care for the sick and poor, many living in slums and huts. Each team had medical and social workers. Most of the funding was raised in India with additional funding sent from the UK when possible. A small van, purchased as a result of the collection of Green Shield Stamps, was sent out from the UK to use for transporting supplies.

Also in the 1960s, in Madras, there was a centre providing training and work for leprosy patients.

IRELAND

Established

1982

History

THE FOUNDATION HAS grown over the years since its inception to be the largest single housing association provider of accommodation for the elderly in the country. The first Sue Ryder House was at Ballyroan, Co Laois (25 units).
There are now centres in:
Kilminchy, Co Laois (70 units)
Dalkey, Co Dublin (48 units)
Holycross, Co Tipperary (36 units)
Nenagh, Co Tipperary (50 units)
Dublin Road, Co Carlow (53 units)

Services provided

Housing schemes for the elderly enabling them to live independently but with many services available.

How funded

State funding, income from Sue Ryder Shops and fund-raising events.

ISRAEL

I N THE LATE 1960s, a Home was established at Nath-
anya to help 26 girls who had been directly or indi-
rectly affected by the aftermath of the Second World
War and the holocaust.

Years later, in Jerusalem, there was a Sue Ryder Foundation Community Care Room provided as part of a
project, Dental Volunteers for Israel—providing proce-
dures for Jewish and Arab children.

ITALY

Established

July 1997

History

IN 1997 SUE Ryder saw the need for palliative care in Italy, and established the charity *Fondazione Sue Ryder,* providing a specialist hospice-palliative care and pain relief service at home free of charge on a 24-hour, 7 day per week basis, together with educational and training events for healthcare professionals and volunteers raising awareness in palliative care and pain relief.

The *Fondazione Sue Ryder* has always worked in some of the most deprived areas of Rome. A Helpline was created in 2017 to give access to information on how families can obtain support and care in Rome. The project has also funded one-off nursing treatments for elderly/ patients in economic difficulty. A network has been created with other voluntary associations and local parishes, exchanging information to identify needs and offer support. People donate medication, healthcare aids etc. which are distributed via the network to families in need.

Fondazione Sue Ryder started a "Coronavirus Emergency Food Bank" project together with the parishes and community groups in April 2020. Packages are distributed twice weekly.

The *Fondazione Sue Ryder* trains volunteers giving information and support for the general public regarding local and regional funding available to them.

How funded

1997–2014 Private donations and Convention with Italian NHS; 2015–2021 Private donations and support from the Lady Ryder of Warsaw Memorial Trust.

Other services

Bereavement service/ volunteer friendship service/ education.

Community work

Working with other charities/ local government for volunteer outreach/ education courses/ local parish network.

Staff engaged at outset, now

1 part time administrator, other professionals paid when needed.

Number of people helped

From July 1997 to December 2020, approximately 6,000, with many more families involved.

MALAWI

Established

1990

History

THE SUE RYDER Foundation in Malawi (SRFIM) is situated in the Southern Region of Malawi, at its own office complex in Balaka Township, opposite Balaka District Hospital out-patient department. SRFIM has provided social and humanitarian support with special emphasis on disadvantaged groups, people with disabilities, epilepsy and asthma.

Services provided

Mainly community services.

How funded

Major funder was Sue Ryder Care (UK). Other donors who have provided financial support include Polish Aid, Czech Aid, Comic Relief, Target TB, Jersey Overseas Aid Commission, DFID, USAID, and Imperial Tobacco Group. Some of the funding is obtained through income-generated activities, particularly through letting out extra office space to other organisations.

Projects

Door to door medical rehabilitation services for persons with physical disabilities from 1990 to 2018.

Community clinics for chronic and neglected conditions of epilepsy and asthma from 1990 to 2018.

Community awareness campaigns on epilepsy (2010–2012).

Community awareness on malaria (2011–2012).

Introduced TB active screening in maternal and child health services in Balaka District targeting children under the age of five and pregnant and lactating mothers (2012–2015).

Currently transitioning to broaden the scope to include environmental challenges, food security, early childhood development, governance, nutrition, Water, Sanitation and Hygiene (WASH) and sustainable development.

Developments and growth

After 10 years of serving Balaka District, the Foundation expanded its services to some parts of the neighbouring Ntcheu District, providing health and medical care on neglected conditions of epilepsy, asthma and physical disabilities to communities which would otherwise be excluded from free government services.

Funds were received from Sue Ryder Care in the UK. Other Sue Ryder organisations such as *Fundacja Sue Ryder* (Poland); *Domov Sue Ryder* (Czech Republic); and Ryder Italia, helped in linking up other supporters from their countries, including Polish Ministry of Foreign Affairs (Polish Aid); Czech Aid; and expert doctors in Italy.

The Foundation in Malawi has proved to be self-sustainable. It has survived a transitional three year period with no external funding.

One invisible but important growth factor is that the Foundation is now moving from service-delivery to community capacity-building and social protection. This approach makes projects more sustainable.

In April 2021, with funds from the Lady Ryder of Warsaw Memorial Trust, a leprosy awareness programme was started with the aim of reducing the cases of leprosy in the country. The programme includes training for health care workers, primary school teachers and non-community health workers, with active screening being promoted to allow for treatment to be given sooner to avoid disability. Community radio stations are also being encouraged to promote screening and the removal of stigma associated with leprosy.

Staff

At the outset there were 14 staff comprising the Director, Accountant, Secretary, data clerk, clinician, nurse, Medical Rehabilitation Technician, driver, three cleaners (including groundsmen), and three security staff.

More recently (2021), there are 10, comprising the Director, Accountant, Programmes Officer, three cleaners (including groundsmen), driver and three security staff. Current projects (when available), make use of existing permanent structures at district and community level which only require improvement in their capacity.

Other comments

Children with disabling conditions, who would otherwise not access education, now attend school. Similarly, adults with disabling conditions, who were solely dependent on family members for survival, now fend for themselves and for their families. This is as a result of medication and physiotherapy services offered by the Foundation.

Myths and superstitious beliefs about epilepsy and physical disabilities have lessened. People in rural communities linked epilepsy and disability with witchcraft, hence instead of seeking medical help, they sought help from traditional witch doctors. Awareness campaigns addressed these myths and communities have begun seeking medical solutions for medical issues.

Number of people helped

Approximately 40,000.

NEPAL

UNDER THE UMBRELLA of the Ryder-Cheshire Foundation, there was a Home for people with physical disabilities. In 2003, it was taken over by another organisation.

NEW ZEALAND

THE RYDER-CHESHIRE FOUNDATION New Zealand, like the Ryder-Cheshire Foundation Australia raises funds to support Raphael in India and Klibur Domin in Timor-Leste. There are also independent Foundations in New Zealand offering care.

Manawatu

The Ryder-Cheshire Foundation Manawatu is a charitable organisation in Hokowhitu, Palmerston North. It was established in 1979 to develop a positive support structure for people with a physical disability. Their mission statement is: "A place to live; a home of one's own."

It is an independent and charitable organisation whose single and dedicated purpose is to ensure people with physical disabilities live as full and active lives as possible.

Whether physically disabled from birth, by accident or illness, adults coming under the care of the Foundation are provided with accommodation, care and support to develop skills, gain confidence and a sufficient level of independence to reach their full potential and enjoy a quality of life.

Support is provided in a complex situated in a well-developed residential area, with easy access to suburban shops, bus route and other amenities.

There are nine specially designed houses on the complex for residents with a variety of physical disabilities. Some are highly dependent. Others live in self-contained units with minimal daily staff assistance, preparing for the day when they might become independent and choose to live elsewhere in the community. The centre also offers short stay accommodation.

Waikato

History

The Ryder-Cheshire Foundation Waikato Charitable Trust was founded in 1987 in response to a community need to support people with disabilities to access rental housing. Fundraising began and the first house was completed in 1991. Since then, seven homes have been built with community funds, with the last five-bedroom home and two-bedroom unit being completed in 2016.

Services provided

The mission is to enhance lives by providing accessible, affordable, quality housing for people with disabilities, to fill the gap between 24-hour care and independence.

The Homes support independent living, with up to five flatmates with a physical or functional disability sharing a home. Residents have a range of conditions including blindness, Multiple Sclerosis, Stroke, accident-related injuries, amputations, Huntington's Disease, Asperger's and Spina Bifida.

Support is available by telephone 24 hours a day.

Residents are assisted to discuss and sort out any flat sharing issues.

Home repairs and maintenance are organised.

Help is given to empower residents who need support within the flat or with outside agencies.

The new flatmate process is managed.

Help is given to co-ordinate individual Carer support to enable people to live as independently as possible.

Support opportunities for resident get-togethers and excursions. These social outings help build friendships and provide fun experiences for residents.

Pursue funding for new housing projects that build the capacity of Ryder-Cheshire Foundation Waikato and provide more social accommodation opportunities for people with disabilities.

How funded

Through grants, donations and from rental and lease income.

Extent of land and homes

The Trust has fundraised and built seven wheelchair accessible homes in Hamilton, housing 28 people.

Beds/rooms:

28 beds in 28 bedrooms

Developments and growth

To build another home—the land is available but funding is needed.

Staff engaged

There is a volunteer Board of Trustees whose sole aim is the wellbeing of the staff and residents. This has created a culture where staff feel engaged with the vision and this has not waned over time, leading to happier, more supported feeling residents.

Number of people helped

Approximately 300 people have been residents in the homes—some of them have been there for 17 years! However, in terms of total people who have benefited from the homes, there will be many more as the residents' families benefit significantly.

Canterbury Ryder-Cheshire Foundation

Inspired by a visit from Sue Ryder and Leonard Cheshire in the 1960s, the Canterbury Ryder-Cheshire Foundation was established to support the work of Raphael, the Ryder-Cheshire Centre in Dehra Dun, India. The fundraising has adapted over the years, becoming more targeted at special projects, with online appeals being made as particular needs at Raphael emerge. The Foundation has also been proactive in attracting skilled volunteers, sometimes the newly retired, to help at Raphael.

In more recent years, the Canterbury RCF has developed links with Klibur Domin, the Ryder-Cheshire Home in Timor-Leste. Along similar lines to supporting Raphael, the Foundation helps with both fundraising and encouraging volunteers to help there.

TIMOR-LESTE

Ryder Cheshire Foundation—Klibur Domin

Established

2000, initiated by Ryder-Cheshire Australia

History

In September 1999, Timor-Leste suffered a major tragedy when armed militia aided by the Indonesian Armed Forces killed over 2000 Timorese people and burnt 80% of all buildings in the country. This traumatic event followed twenty-four years of brutal occupation by Indonesia during which an estimated 240,000 people lost their lives. Ryder-Cheshire Australia decided to assist the Timorese people by establishing a home for sick and disabled people. It was named Klibur Domin (Sharing with Love).

Services provided

Detection and treatment of Tuberculosis and Multi-Drug Resistant TB (MDR-TB).

Six Inpatient wards for TB, MDR-TB, Kidney Dialysis, Strokes, Wounds, Fractures, Malaria, Malnutrition etc.

A Mental Health Ward for six females.

Three Mobile TB Outreach Teams detecting and treating TB in remote villagers.

A Mobile Outreach Team treating people with disabilities in remote villages.

A Medical Clinic treating outpatients from Tibar and surrounding areas.

A Dental Clinic treating people from Tibar and school-children in surrounding villages.

A Medical Facility in Baucau (Timor-Leste's second largest city) for the detection and treatment of TB and MDR-TB.

A Respite Centre offering people with disabilities from remote areas medical care and support.

A Rehab Centre providing Physiotherapy and Occupational Therapy to patients and Respite Centre clients.

A home for ten children with disabilities from remote villages who attend the secondary school across the road.

Klibur Domin in Timor Leste

Funding

Ryder-Cheshire Australia provides an amount each year towards operating costs and has provided more than a million dollars over the twenty years, 2000–2020.

The Global Fund (a fund contributed to by governments worldwide and the private sector specifically for projects to combat AIDS, TB and malaria) provides funds annually for TB and MDR-TB.

The Timorese Ministry of Social Security and Inclusion (MSSI) contributes annually for disability services.

The Korean Office of International Cooperation (KOICA) is currently funding the Baucau TB operation.

Further income has come from Rotary, Foreign Embassies and other donors.

Extent of land and homes

The land area of Klibur Domin is approximately ten hectares and there are now twenty buildings on the site.

Beds/rooms

There are 85 beds for patients and residents and another 15 beds for international volunteers.

Other services

Klibur Domin has seven vehicles and twelve motor bikes. Five vehicles are 4WD and used to travel to remote mountain villages. One is a 15- seater bus used for administration and transporting patients to and from the Dili Hospital. One is a 4WD ambulance used when patients need to be transported in the reclining position.

Number of communal rooms

Eight—each ward has a communal room and there is a large communal room in the Respite Centre. There are also external shaded facilities where patients and residents can gather.

Community work

Klibur Domin works very closely with the local Tibar community, providing outpatient clinical and dental care and transport to the Dili Hospital for sick people and mothers in labour. It works closely with villagers through its outreach programs, constructing ramps and ablution facilities where needed.

Developments and growth

Since its establishment, Klibur Domin has undergone continuous expansion and improvement to become the excellent facility that it is today. In recent years to supplement Klibur Domin's food supply, vegetable gardens and fruit trees have been established and livestock are being introduced. The latest project has seen 132 solar panels and nine Tesla batteries installed so that Klibur Domin will be independent of the unreliable and expensive grid power.

Klibur Domin has become the premier facility in Timor-Leste detecting and treating TB and MDR-TB. It also has an excellent reputation in the care of people with disabilities. It is highly respected by the Timorese Government and other NGOs.

UKRAINE

IN 1996, SUE Ryder was invited by the Society of Polish Culture in Rowne to meet members of the Polish community in the city. Until the Second World War, Rowne had belonged to Poland. Sue witnessed the extreme poverty in the city and as a start, a soup kitchen was opened by nuns with assistance from the Foundation.

UNITED KINGDOM

T HERE ARE A number of varied activities which were started by Sue Ryder and many continue to exist in the UK. This section lists them. They are the neurological care centres, hospices and bereavement support services operated under Sue Ryder (previously known as Sue Ryder Care). There were support groups and there are retreat houses and of course the memorial trust known as the Lady Ryder of Warsaw Memorial Trust.

Sue Ryder Homes

From the first Home in Cavendish, Suffolk in the 1950s, there followed many more. Although some have now closed as needs have changed, listed below are the Homes which were opened and the care provided there.

Opened in the 1950s—1990s they were open for varying lengths of time, some for many years but have since closed.

Acorn Bank

Near Penrith, Cumbria. Disabled and some elderly. 27 beds.

Binny House

Ecclesmachan, West Lothian. For people with physical disabilities, plus respite and terminal care. 31 beds.

Birchley Hall

Billinge, near Wigan, Lancashire. Disabled and frail elderly. 23 beds.

Bordean House

Near Petersfield, Hampshire. 14 beds for the elderly and 10 for patients with cancer, convalescent and terminal.

Cavendish

Suffolk. For the physically disabled, medical and terminal. 30 beds.

Cuerden Hall

Bamber Bridge, Lancashire. General chronic sick and very physically disabled. Respite and terminal care. Long and short term care. 37 beds.

Hickleton Hall

Near Doncaster, Yorkshire. Physically handicapped and frail elderly. Day Care and Domiciliary service. 53 beds.

Holme Hall

Holme-on-Spalding Moor, East Yorkshire. For physically disabled. Elderly frail, Huntington's Disease, physiotherapy, day care services. 45 beds.

Marchmont House

Berwickshire. For people with physical disabilities, including those with Huntington's Disease and other neurological diseases. 36 beds.

Nettlebed

Oxfordshire. For palliative care, respite and terminal care. Domiciliary and bereavement visits. Day Centre. 25 beds.

Staunton Harold Hall

Ashby-de-la-Zouch, Leicestershire. Providing palliative care and support. Day Centre. Domiciliary and respite care. 20 beds.

The Old Hall, Snettisham

Norfolk. Physically disabled and elderly. Respite care. 28 beds.

The Old Palace

Ely, Cambridgeshire. For residents with varying disabilities, including a small Huntington's Disease wing, beds for long stay and respite care. 45 beds.

The Old Vicarage, Walsingham

Norfolk. Frail elderly and those with mental health conditions. 30 beds.

Wembley

A short stay home for 8 young mentally handicapped children, especially to give relief to hard-pressed parents.

Wootton House

Sheffield, South Yorkshire. Half-way house for patients with mental health problems. 13 beds.

During the 1970s and 1980s, there were various initiatives in London to provide housing for those who were homeless.

The following centres were opened in Sue Ryder's lifetime and the work continues there today

Sue Ryder St John's Hospice

In Moggerhanger in Bedfordshire, and provides expert care for life-limiting conditions, with everything from pain and symptom management to emotional and practical help.

Sue Ryder Manorlands Hospice

In Oxenhope, near Keighley. As well as expert palliative care, support is given to people with life-limiting conditions. Working across Airedale, Wharfedale, Craven and Bradford.

Sue Ryder Leckhampton Court Hospice

In Cheltenham, Gloucestershire. Provides an inpatient unit for specialist palliative care. Care is also given in people's own homes or people can visit for Day Services.

Stagenhoe

A Sue Ryder specialist neurological care centre based in Hertfordshire, caring for people aged 18 and over with a range of neurological conditions such as Huntington's Disease, Parkinson's and Multiple Sclerosis.

The Chantry

A Sue Ryder specialist neurological care centre based in Ipswich, Suffolk caring for people aged 18 and over with a range of neurological conditions such as Huntington's Disease, Parkinson's and Multiple Sclerosis.

Sue Ryder Thorpe Hall Hospice

The only specialist palliative care inpatient unit in Peterborough. Provides care and support for people living with life-limiting conditions.

Sue Ryder Wheatfields Hospice

In Headingley, Leeds, providing expert palliative care and support for people with a life-limiting condition.

New centres which have started since Sue Ryder's death

Dee View Court

A Sue Ryder specialist neurological care centre based in Aberdeen, caring for people aged 18 and over with a range of neurological conditions such as Huntington's Disease and Multiple Sclerosis.

Sue Ryder Neurological Care Centre Lancashire

A purpose-built, state of the art neurological care centre based in Eastway, Preston, providing specialist neurological support and rehabilitation tailored to the individual needs of people with a range of neurological conditions.

Sue Ryder Duchess of Kent Hospice

Offers a range of services in Berkshire from three sites: Duchess of Kent Hospice, Wokingham Day Hospice and Sue Ryder Palliative Care Hub Berkshire. Hospice at Home care in the community.

Sue Ryder's Scottish Homecare services

Based in Stirling and supporting people across Stirling, Falkirk, Perth and Clackmannanshire. Offering care for people with life-changing conditions such as Multiple Sclerosis, Parkinson's disease, stroke and dementia.

Sue Ryder Palliative Care Hub South Oxfordshire

Provides Hospice at Home care in the community.

Sue Ryder Shops

At the time of Sue Ryder's death there were 500 Sue Ryder shops in the UK. Sue Ryder described them as the lifeblood of the Foundation. They supported the work in the UK and overseas, and she visited them individually each year.

Sue Ryder Support Groups

Throughout the UK, as well as the network of Sue Ryder Shops, from the 1960s–1990s, there were many Support Groups organising fundraising events, giving talks, selling Christmas cards and gifts. Many of these were later absorbed into the Sue Ryder Shops network, or under the fundraising of the individual Homes/Care Centres/Hospices, and the remaining few were wound up after many years of incredible support.

Sue Ryder Holiday Scheme

In the late 1960s the holiday scheme for survivors from the concentration camps which had operated in Denmark was transferred to England and groups of 35, mainly Poles, were welcomed at Long Melford Hall in Suffolk, part of which Sue Ryder leased from the National Trust. The Foundation then acquired Stagenhoe near Hitchin in

Hertfordshire as a base for the scheme. Six groups came most years for three weeks at a time. Sue Ryder had to invite each one personally so they could obtain permission from the communist government in Poland to leave the country. They went on various sight-seeing trips and loved their time in England, escaping the grim times being experienced in their own country.

Sue Ryder Retreat Houses and the Sue Ryder Prayer Fellowship

Sue Ryder's Christian faith was immensely important to her. In 1984, she established the *Sue Ryder Prayer Fellowship* to be a "powerhouse of prayer" for the needs of others and for the worldwide work carried out in her name.

The Martyrs House, Walsingham

Norfolk—a small retreat house providing accommodation to pilgrims and visitors to Walsingham was open from the 1980s until 2000.

St Katharine's, Parmoor

Near Henley on Thames—a Retreat House owned and run by the *Sue Ryder Prayer Fellowship*, offering Quiet Days and Retreats with accommodation for up to 36 people. The House was given to Sue Ryder by Mother Christine, the last surviving member of the Community of St Katharine of Alexandria which had owned the house for over 50 years.

St Katharine's is also home to the Lady Ryder Memorial Garden, situated in the walled garden of the House, run entirely by volunteers. It has a sensory area for visitors with disabilities and each week, about 30 children with Special Needs visit the Memorial Garden to help with different tasks.

Lady Ryder of Warsaw Memorial Trust

Established by Sue Ryder in 2000, initially as the Bouverie Foundation, to continue the work overseas. A few years after Sue Ryder's death, the name was changed to the Lady Ryder of Warsaw Memorial Trust. In line with Sue Ryder's vision, the Trust has a presence in Lourdes, having worked with the Polish Catholic Mission in creating rooms especially for those who are disabled to stay with their family/carers. Over the years, significant support has been given to Poland—particularly to a new Home at Pierzchnica—and to the ongoing work in Italy. More recently, the Trust is pleased to have been able to help the Foundation in Malawi.

In 2020 the Trust provided emergency funding to seven Homes in Poland and to *Fondazione Sue Ryder* in Italy to help with the purchase of emergency supplies in the wake of the Coronavirus pandemic.

The Trust has also welcomed applications for funding from other organisations where they are carrying out work with limited funds and where the funding from the Trust will really make a difference.

In 2021 a major initiative was launched in preparation to mark the Centenary. Medical Scholarships have been awarded to students at Bristol and Newcastle Universities to help train more doctors. Although medical students are eligible for grants and student loans while training, those who come from disadvantaged backgrounds often face financial difficulties and may be unable to embark on such a course and career. To date, significant funds have already been granted to support five students and it is planned to increase this number year by year, provided that enough funds can be raised.

FORMER YUGOSLAVIA

S UE RYDER STARTED working with the health authorities in Yugoslavia in the 1950/60s and Professor M Andrejevic, a specialist in geriatrics drew her attention to the need to establish units in the city hospital in Belgrade. These Homes were subsequently established in Belgrade, for different age groups and comprised two medical units and one surgical unit, together with a centre for physiotherapy and occupational therapy for patients who otherwise would be blocking hospital beds.

At the same time, in the 1950s, 1960s and 1970s, the building of other Homes started in different parts of the country on the same basis as in Poland—in co-operation with the local and national health authorities, with many of the homes being prefabricated buildings shipped out from the UK.

In the 1980s a Sue Ryder Shop opened in Kotor in Montenegro to raise funds.

By the time of Sue Ryder's death in 2000, there were Homes in the following locations. In some places two or more Homes were located in one place.

Croatia

Gospic—2 homes
Velika—3 homes, caring for 139 people

Serbia

Belgrade—2 homes, including one for babies
Kragujevac—2 homes

Bosnia and Herzegovina

Travnik—2 homes
Mostar—2 homes—we believe these were destroyed during the break-up of Yugoslavia in the early 1990s.

Kosovo

Pristina—2 homes

Montenegro

Risan—4 homes caring for 300 people

North Macedonia

Bitola—2 homes caring for over 120 people
Bansko—home for children

Since Sue Ryder's death, a Hospice has been opened in Skopje, North Macedonia.

At the time her autobiography was revised in 1997 Sue Ryder estimated that 60,000 people had received care in the Homes in Yugoslavia.

ADDENDUM

Under the umbrella of the Ryder-Cheshire Foundation, in the 1990s, there was a rehabilitation centre in the Mpanda District of Tanzania and a Home for 34 disabled children in Papua New Guinea.

INFORMATION SOURCES
FOR PART TWO

1. Sue Ryder's autobiography, *Child of My Love*.

2. Issues of the annual magazine of the Sue Ryder Foundation, *Remembrance*.

3. The individual Foundations overseas and/or from their websites.

AFTERWORD

J UST BEFORE HER death, Sue Ryder formed the
Bouverie Foundation to continue her work, looking
after the various overseas foundations she had
undertaken in the previous fifty years. The name was later
changed to the Lady Ryder of Warsaw Memorial Trust
(LRWMT) and we continue to do this work on her behalf
by providing necessary funds, holding her legacy dear.

The trustees are delighted to present this publication,
marking the centenary of Sue Ryder's birth (July 1924)
which includes a review of the areas where Sue worked
across the world, completed by Ruth Young, our administrator, who worked with Sue.

The LRWMT has, as part of the centenary, created a
Medical Scholarship, helping students wishing to train in
the medical profession as a doctor, nurse or other health
worker, with the necessary funds to fulfil their training.
This scholarship is just beginning and it will be long
lasting. The Trust has signed two agreements with leading
universities in Britain. It puts medical professionals in the
field, it helps social mobility and above all is potentially
life-changing for the many people who will receive care
from these young medics over the years. The recipients of
these scholarships will be selected by the universities as
outstanding scholars with real potential.

The Trust is also open to other grant applicants. Our
aims are:

- first, to help the Sue Ryder overseas family to continue
  Sue's work,

- and also, to help any smaller charity where a modest amount of money will make a significant difference. This follows Sue's own ethos: she liked to urge people to "help the person in front of you" rather than indulge in grandiose schemes.

Over the last five years, nearly £500,000 has been awarded by LRWMT, to projects in Poland and other countries including Britain. In 2020–21 the Trust was able to fund projects associated with the challenges presented by the COVID-19 outbreak and also the Ukrainian refugee crisis.

We are proud in what we do in Sue's name and to continue her legacy. Our website gives further information about our work: www.lrwmt.org.uk

For the cause that lacks assistance,
the wrong that needs resistance,
for the future in the distance
and the good that I can do.

George Linnaeus Banks

Sue Ryder's work must not be forgotten.

Robert Frith FCA
Chairman,
The Lady Ryder of Warsaw Memorial Trust
info@lrwmt.org.uk
www.lrwmt.org.uk
Registered Charity No. 1082295
Company registered in England and Wales No. 03935283

SELECT BIBLIOGRAPHY

Baroness Ryder of Warsaw Sue Ryder. *Child Of My Love.* Revised Edition. London: The Harvill Press, 1997.

Beslièvre, June, and Peter F. Russell. *"Still the Candle Burns": An Anthology of Reminiscences and Reflections on Group Captain Leonard Cheshire VC OM DSO DFC Contributed by Some of His Many Friends from across the World.* St Helier: Jersey Cheshire Home Foundation, 1997.

Bethell, Nicholas William. *The Last Secret: Forcible Repatriation to Russia, 1944-7.* London: Deutsch, 1974.

Dickens, Monica. *One Pair of Feet.* Harmondsworth: Penguin, 1976.

Forrest, Alec John. *But Some There Be.* London: R. Hale, 1957.

Grehan, John, and Martin Mace. *Unearthing Churchill's Secret Army: The Official List of SOE Casualties and Their Stories.* Barnsley: Pen and Sword Military, 2012.

Morris, Richard. *Cheshire: The Biography of Leonard Cheshire, VC, OM.* London: Penguin, 1999.

Tolstoy, Nikolai. *Victims of Yalta: The Secret Betrayal of the Allies: 1944-1947.* New York: Pegasus Books, 2012.

Walker, Jonathan. *Poland Alone: Britain, SOE and the Collapse of the Polish Resistance,1944.* Stroud: The History Press, 2011.

West, Tessa. *Lady Sue Ryder of Warsaw: Single-Minded Philanthropist.* Chicago: Shepheard-Walwyn, 2019.

Wolkowinska, Cecylia, and Joanna Bogle. *When the Summer Ended: One Woman's War Story.* Leominster: Gracewing, 1992.